Chalkdust Memories

Lessons from a Teaching Career

Dana Dunnan

Random Recollections House www.chalkdustmemories.com Walden, Vermont

ISBN-13: 978-1492320074
ISBN-10: 1492320072

For Judy

I am the moon to her sun. Whatever shine I have is a product of the light she gives off. She is why I rise every day, filled with the newness of morning.

Books by Dana Dunnan

Burning at the Grassroots: Inside the Dean Machine

Wrestling with the Past: Life In and Out of the Ring

(with Paul "Butcher" Vachon)

Chalkdust Memories; Lessons from a Teaching Career

Notes to a New Teacher; A Not-for Dummies Guide for Beginning Teachers

Table of Contents

Foreword: Forewarned

This is not a work of fiction. It is a work of perception, of all the perceptions I had that formed my reality as a teacher.

In making measurements in science, there is a phenomenon called parallax. The angle you view a measurement from, say, the curve of liquid in a thermometer or buret, affects the reading you record. Similarly, in all of the shots of Sylvester Stallone in the *Rocky* movies, the camera was angled upward. While Stallone could pharmaceutically enhance his bulk to heavyweight level for the movies, only the camera could make him seem taller.

So my work has its own parallax issues. It is entirely from my angle.

Most of the people portrayed here were significantly older than I was. Since I'm in my sixties now, many of them may have passed on already. Some of the people portrayed in the book who are still around might not like how I perceived them. I have not identified most adults with full names, although anyone with a modicum of research skills could find out who they are.

I chose pseudonyms and first names for teachers, and altered last names for administrators. When I began teaching, I was reluctant to address administrators by their first names, because I respected their positions. My father and both brothers were administrators, and, regardless of any familial conflicts, I respected the work they did.

For students, I have changed names if anything I am saying might reflect badly upon or embarrass them.

In writing this book, I've struggled some with the tone. I've utilized footnotes a lot to provide the reader with some options.

Many people think the book <u>Infinite Jest</u> is a masterpiece. When I read it, I was initially fascinated with the use of footnotes to expand upon the story. As I got further into the book, I saw that David Foster Wallace even used lengthy footnotes to create whole new story lines.

By the end of the book, the footnotes annoyed the hell out of me. Turning to the back of the book all of the time, for something that might be illuminating, or might be completely tangential, lost its charm.[1] Therefore, I'm using footnotes that are usually on the same page as what they reference; if not they show up on the next page.

When I started writing this, I wasn't using footnotes at all. Then I found that there were books and articles I wanted an interested reader to be able to find.

I also decided to use footnotes to moderate the tone of the book somewhat. I am inherently a smartass. In most conversations, I will inject attempts at humor along the way.

---

[1] Wallace was institutionalized during his short life, and, ultimately, committed suicide. In literature, the line between genius and insanity is sometimes blurry. I think I probably fall some distance from either side of that line. Like, somewhat insightful and moderately quirky, we'll say.

Some people might not appreciate my particular humor, so I'm using footnotes to put humor in a place where it can be ignored if you don't have any interest.

Much of the book is oral history I've been hauling around for years. Some of it is soapbox oratory that I've long imposed upon listeners, both willing and otherwise. All of the writing is meant to be in a comfortable and conversational style. Of course, in writing, my word selection, sentence structure, development of ideas, and overall coherence is better than I could manage if I was just talking to you.

My hope is that I am able to convey the culture in which I worked. Schools change, evolve, improve, and decline. The Masconomet Regional High School that is central to this memoir doesn't even exist anymore. The year I finished teaching, they were finalizing a new building. That was 13 years ago, enough time for a new generation of teachers to help shape a different culture from the one upon which I reflect.

My reflections include a fair dose of cynicism. If I've constructed this memoir correctly, the reasons for the cynicism will be readily evident.

Consider yourself warned.

Chapter 1

Getting Schooled

I come from a family of educators. My father and both brothers started out as teachers. All three left the classroom and went into management in public or private schools.

When I started my career, I expected to make the same move from classroom to administration, and the quicker, the better. Fortunately for me, I found enough joy in the classroom that I never left, until the day I left school behind me.

Families of firemen and cops tend to produce new generations in the same profession. In my family, the success of my father and brothers was something to guide my aspirations. When my father talked about why he had moved into administration, he said that he had felt as a classroom teacher that he had to be able to do a principal's or superintendent's job better than the people he saw in those positions.

I don't know if I got the same attitude from nature, nurture, or experience.

Humility is highly over-rated.

My family's history in Exeter, New Hampshire, goes back nearly as far as that of Phillips Exeter Academy. My mother's family built a 17-room Federalist home in the very center of town in

1826[2]. At various times in that century, Academy students boarded in the house.

My great uncle, Perley Gardner, a brilliant, odd-looking, and painfully shy individual, attended the Academy near the end of the 19th century. Some two decades later, a bachelor lawyer living with a mother who was on the road to crazy, he adopted my mother so that she would not be placed in an orphanage by a mother who couldn't care for her.

My mother grew up in the big old house, entertaining boys from the academy in the front parlor as she entered adolescence. Her memories of that childhood were not terribly fond ones. But we still went back to Exeter during summers in my

---

[2] For $6000 and "rum for the workers."

childhood, to visit with Perley, who now rambled around the house alone.

As I was entering high school, my father, and my godfather, Dana Cotton, sat me down to talk about how I should plan to go to Harvard. Dana Cotton had known my dad since their days together at UNH. My father had gone to UNH on an athletic scholarship. Dana Cotton was sort of a bag man. As manager of the football team, he carried around a satchel containing money, which could be distributed to players like my dad, when they indicated a need[3].

Dana Cotton ended up at Harvard, in the School of Education, where he was head of the division that found jobs for Ed school grads. My father got his doctorate at Harvard, and Dana Cotton was integral in advancing my father's career from one superintendency to the next. When Harvard would be asked for candidates for an open superintendency, Dana would forward my father's name first, if it was a job he wanted[4].

Getting my name from Dana Cotton, my godfather, was weighted with expectations.

---

[3] I suspect the statute of limitations on an NCAA investigation has expired.

[4] One of the last jobs for which my Dad was a candidate was the superintendency in Oakland, California. While I was at Stanford, the Oakland superintendent was assassinated. His killers were the Symbionese Liberation Army, the same revolutionaries who kidnapped Patty Hearst. The Oakland superintendent was African-American. Those were some confused revolutionaries.

These were expectations I was clearly not headed toward fulfilling while I was in high school. Therefore, the discussion between my father and godfather was how to make me a better candidate for acceptance at Harvard.

For all you fans of irony, there are a couple of ingots here. First is that my father, whose field was education, was not a particularly good analyst of how to motivate his son. My lackluster report cards caused him to say, on more than one occasion, that, at my current rate, I would be lucky to get into Mankato State Teachers' College. Rather than inspiring me, that made me feel he was predicting the level at which I belonged. He was, after all, the superintendent of schools.

The second ingot didn't show up until long after my father's death, when we were plowing through his old papers. My father went to Everett High School, just before the Depression. Everett was a fairly poor town next to Boston, and the high school was probably not great. My father went to UNH on an athletic scholarship, not an academic scholarship. His high school grades were far worse than mine.

Anyway, in the mid-Sixties, Phillips Exeter was still an all-boys school. The idea was floated that I might attend there, and I resolutely rejected it, having found a greater interest in the opposite sex than in academic achievement.

My godfather proposed that the next best thing might be my going to Summer School at the Academy. When I found out that the Summer School included females, I made the concession to apply.

The application I submitted as a sophomore must have been thoroughly unimpressive. I remember that I wrote an essay in which I posited that the Academy ought to be selling me on why I should go there, rather than the other way around.

Clearly, they didn't buy that argument. I was rejected.

That was a good experience to have at that age, since it got my attention. Although I was no ball of fire, I applied myself somewhat more in my junior year[5]. My application for the summer of 1968 was accepted.

It was the best summer of my young life. The wealth of resources at the Academy was amazing. There were sports with good coaches, classes with teachers from the Academy as well as other good high schools, excursions, and girls.

Dominican girls from New York City, Jewish girls from Long Island, blondes from California; and all of them were smart. And here, being intelligent wasn't a social negative, as it was in many of my high school's social circles.

That didn't mean I knocked myself out in my classes. My father had picked two of them, a math course and a biology course. I was allowed to pick an English course.

Of the three grades given, Honors, Satisfactory, and Unsatisfactory, I got three Satisfactorys.

---

[5] All my life, I was the youngest student in my grade. It didn't help that I wasn't burdened with an excess of maturity. Not excusing, just explaining.

Right in that meaty part of the curve.

Of course, giving me a lower grade may have been more hassle than my teachers cared to endure.

Regardless of my effort, the surroundings that summer changed my view of my own potential.

Which is exactly why I came to understand how tracking can relegate students to expectations that will forever limit their potential.

Although I had generally been in advanced classes, I had always felt that it was because of my father's position. In the advanced classes, I was the bottom of the class, along with my friend Burke[6], who was more commonly called Butch[7], although we did lead the class in inappropriate behavior.

I didn't think my father's position was what got me admitted to the Phillips Exeter Summer School, since they had rejected me the previous year[8].

Surrounded by smart, accomplished kids who had high expectations, both imposed upon them and for themselves, changed how I viewed myself.

---

[6] When I told my father I had a friend named Burke, he said to my mother that the name sounded like a fart in the bathtub. Dad rose mightily in my eyes for that insight.

[7] Butch- now there's a big improvement. It sounded like he was a character in the Our Gang comedies.

[8] I realize now that Dana Cotton may have exerted a little more influence that second summer. I'm glad that didn't occur to me then.

It was a great summer[9].

In my less-than-stellar academic career in high school and college, I only got one grade below a C. That was a D+ in Calculus at UNH.

Two semesters of Calculus were required for my Chemistry major. The instructor in that first semester of Calculus was well into his dotage. His hearing was bad enough that students stopped asking questions after the first few classes, since he never heard the question as it was asked anyhow.

So the calculus kinda lost me- more even than anything in my chemistry courses, where C's were pretty common on my record. The D+ came first semester of my sophomore year. So I hatched a brilliant proposal for my parents.

I would go back to Minnesota for the summer, take that second course at the U of M, and then I could really focus on improving.

Of course, I had an ulterior motive. My high school friends from Minnesota[10] were having a grand time. They were slowly dissipating the potential their lives held, occasionally getting arrested for annoying the authorities in any number of ways,

---

[9] I also got to know a kid from Hanover who would introduce me to my future wife when we went to UNH.

[10] They included Marvin the car thief, Paul the pyromaniac, and Butch the petty thief. In the senior yearbook, they finished in a dead heat for "Most Likely to be Outlined in Chalk".

and living together in a house that was probably somewhere below Board of Health standards.

This sounded like a great time to me, although I think I was wise enough that I agreed to stay in a dorm at the U. Probably at my parents' insistence, in fact.

And I wouldn't have a car, so seeing my friends in St. Paul when the U was in Minneapolis would be more problematic.

As soon as I got to my room at the U, I found a place where I could purchase a bike that I could sell back at the end of the term.

I found out that first day that it was a really long ride to see my friends, but it was certainly worth it for the cultural enrichment.

The first day of my calculus class, the instructor walked in and may have initially gone unrecognized, because he looked the same age as the students, and had hair at least as long as most, and longer than many.

A promising sign.

As he spoke up describing the class, he said he wanted it to be an experiment.

This was another promising sign.

He said he wanted to teach calculus the way we would find most useful. And that we should decide how the course was graded.

He really had everyone's attention now.

We could choose whether he would use traditional grading, or we could assign our own grades, or he could give everyone an A.

Ding,ding,ding,ding,ding,ding!!!!!

The class voted, and, undoubtedly driven by principles of egalitarianism, we voted for everyone to receive an A.

This seemed too good to be true.

As class, and the summer, went on, I started a pattern of heading over to St. Paul on my bike every afternoon.

Things didn't really start to get interesting until well after dark, so I was spending many a late summer night pedaling back to my dorm.

And the calculus class wasn't really clearing the fog of my understanding of the subject.

Of course, that may have been impacted by the fact that it began at the grueling hour of 10 AM, which was too early a start for someone participating in the Tour de Minnesota.

So, the summer wore on, and my attendance became rather spotty.

Then the course was over, and I returned to the family home in Exeter, hoping the instructor kept his promise.

When the grade report came, I intercepted it before my parents could see it.

And there it was: an A! I showed my parents and let them shower me with praise for my summer's efforts.

It was at least a decade before I told them the true story.

And I never saw calculus get used- not in any of my college chemistry courses, not in any of the many high school chemistry texts I examined.

And certainly not in my classroom.

So I don't feel too guilty about that A.

When I went out to Stanford to interview for what seemed a long shot for graduate school, I also went to UCLA.

I was attending a basketball coaching clinic there. UCLA was reigning national champion, and Bill Walton had been national player of the year. The coach of the UCLA men, John Wooden, may have been the best college basketball coach ever, and he certainly was the most successful.

In addition, and not coincidentally, John Wooden was also a truly great human being. An All-American in basketball as a player himself, his knowledge of the game was exceeded by his understanding of human beings. His kind, grandfatherly appearance was backed by a steel will and total self-control.[11] His books on dealing with players, and life in general, are wonderful.

Bill Walton was, and is, a bright, verbal, and complex individual. He was a severe stutter into his adult years, and has overcome that to become an overly-verbal sportscaster today. He may

---

[11] Wooden never, ever swore. I occasionally try to eliminate swearing from my vocabulary. The effort usually lasts hours, at best.

have been the best player ever in men's college basketball. He probably grew to 7'3", but always insisted on being listed as 6'11 ½", because he didn't want to be viewed as a freakish seven foot giant.

So, when I got to Wooden's coaching clinic, the difficulty of dealing with his best player was common knowledge. Therefore, when Wooden had finished speaking, I went up and asked him how he could treat Bill Walton differently than his other players.

Wooden's initial comment was that if I was on his basketball team, I would get my haircut. Then he said, "I treat Bill Walton differently because he is Bill Walton. I don't try to treat my players the same, I treat them fairly."

Wooden's flexibility in dealing with Walton was undoubtedly a key to Walton's success in college. It would later come out that Wooden knowingly allowed Walton to use marijuana, which Walton maintained eased the pain in his knees.

Wooden also showed that knowing how someone will react to discipline is enormously helpful. Before a season when UCLA stood as reigning champion, Walton came to Wooden with really long hair. He told the coach that he really liked his long hair and that he wouldn't cut it.

Wooden responded that he admired the depth of Bill's conviction, and that it had been really wonderful having him with the program. He wished him good luck, since he was obviously choosing to leave the program, and shook his hand.

A shorn Walton entered the coach's office the next day, and begged to be allowed back in the program. Wooden acquiesced, and Walton had another dominant year on the court.

And I cut my hair after meeting John Wooden.

One of the courses I took in teacher training at Stanford was educational psychology. It was taught by Dave Berliner, who was a national leader in the field. He was working that year with Nate Gage on a text that would be widely used in educational psychology courses[12]. In his course, Berliner talked a great deal about test design. At the bottom of the hierarchy of types of test questions resided the multiple choice question.

While I fully agreed with his deprecations of multiple choice, it was probably my skill at such questions that got me admitted to Berkeley as an undergrad (I went to UNH instead, and for a multitude of reasons, starting with my future wife, could not have been better situated). I got great SAT, and, later, GRE, scores. It certainly wasn't a sterling academic record that helped my admissions chances.

One thing in Berliner's course that really interested me was correlational studies. When I found that data could be crunched to provide a number that would show a positive or negative correlation and the degree of that correlation, I was entranced.

Talking with the teacher under whom I was doing my teaching internship, he mentioned that he had always felt that there was a high correlation between students being good in music and good in chemistry.

So I acquired grades in those subjects for a large number of students at Woodside High, where I was teaching, and crunched the numbers. There it was: the correlation was positive and very high. I think I did other subject/grade correlations and found much lower correlation, although I think it was still positive.

---

[12] Berliner and Gage, Educational Psychology

Pleased with myself, I wrote this all up in a paper and shared it with Berliner, even though no papers were assigned in the course. He loved it. He wrote a huge A+ on the front and commented at great length. (I told him that, as a kid, the grade on the top of that paper might have made the walk home more hazardous than usual. He said he had experienced a similar childhood.)

The assessment done in his ed psych course consisted exclusively of…………….

Wait for it………..

Wait for it…………..

Multiple choice tests!

Therefore, although I was finally getting my academic ass in gear by graduate school, I didn't exactly kill myself preparing for those tests.

My grade in the course?

An A minus!

When I asked why I received the grade, I was told that grades were based strictly on the tests.

Before the next quarter started, I got a call from one of the professor's assistants in the ed psych course. Because of the great paper I had done, the professor wanted me to be a teaching assistant.

Being this was Stanford, I think I just laughed when I said "no".

The efficiency of multiple choice questions is why they have predominated in forms of national assessment, at all levels of education. A true portrait of a students' mastery might be produced by having a portfolio for each subject. Like most economic decisions, if you want something that is better, it is going to cost more.

Critics bemoan the nature of national testing, but the true bottom line is that if we were committed to better assessment, we would have to make a larger economic commitment to education.

If we are a nation truly committed to equal opportunity for all, and to a vibrant democracy with full participation by all, we need a national curriculum, and the economic commitment to our schools to assess that it works.

My personal understanding of test anxiety came courtesy of the Stanford Graduate School of Education. I had never had test anxiety, partly because I usually didn't care all that deeply how I did. I truly believe that everything has been recorded in my memory, and that finding a deep enough level of relaxation will always allow the correct answer to come forth.

I've always known that trying too hard could effectively block my memory. Sitting around with friends, we would labor over something truly important, like who sang "Purple People Eater"? Great effort would produce no results. So, an hour later, when I was not thinking about it at all, I would blurt out, "Sheb Wooley!"[13]

The first day of the teacher preparation program at Stanford, we stood around chatting informally before we were called together in a large circle of desks. The head of the program introduced himself, and told us a little bit about himself. Then he had us go around the room, repeating the process he had modeled for us.

When we finished the circle, he said, "Now, if you can't remember the name of every person who just introduced themselves, you probably shouldn't be teaching."

I was struck by a panic exceeded only once before in my life.[14] I looked around the circle at people who had just said their names. The names of those I hadn't chatted up before we started raced from my mind at light speed. That created a partial vacuum, which then sucked out the handful I had met before we sat in circle.

---

[13] Impressed? I knew you would be. Now, if I could just find my reading glasses.

[14] When my Dad, who was supposed to be in Chicago, came around the corner of the refrigerator, as I stood at the kitchen sink, holding a beer in my tenth grade hands.
"Dad, you're supposed to be in Chicago!"
"Well, I'm NOT!"

There may have been ten people around that circle. There may have been thirty. For any number between two and infinity, I had no names. I probably could have retrieved them all, but only under hypnosis.[15]

I thought, "I'm <u>so</u> screwed."

And, ever since then, I've been very poor at names. Which, of course becomes a self-fulfilling prophesy.

So, I fully understand test anxiety.[16]

---

[15] Which would have dredged up those memories of being probed by the aliens.

[16] My first year of teaching, I photocopied student pictures from the school yearbook so I could create a photographic seating chart for each class. After that, my anxiety abated enough that I just used the traditional names on seating charts.

Chapter 2

Getting Started in the Classroom

On my first full-time teaching job, when I was exclusively a chemistry teacher, I taught five classes in a seven period day. I was the only newcomer in the department, and everyone else taught four classes. All the other members of the science department had their own classrooms, while I taught in three different rooms, in three different wings of the building. Each room "belonged" to someone else, with all the territoriality that implies. Each room had a teaching aide, whom the teacher in that room usually treated as theirs exclusively.

By that June, I was exhausted. Having failed to leave time for exercise, my back was killing me.[17] It is not hard to see why so many people leave the profession in the first three years.

After seven years in science, I got laid off from that department. I had the option of bumping my way into the English department. I was so pissed off at being bumped out of science that I took a year's leave of absence.

Having no kids, and a wife who was a public school speech pathologist , I could afford the time off. It rejuvenated me,

---

[17] When I went to a doctor for an analysis of my back, he said I would need back surgery, and that I could probably never play basketball again. I spent the summer doing hundreds of sit-ups daily, and the back problem dissipated. I did, in the process, so strengthen my back muscles that, under great stress, my back would tighten up and torture me.

allowed me to spend months with my father as he recovered from an amputation, and gave me the energy to wade into the English department.

While I did get my own room, I also got the journalism course, a grammar/vocabulary course, and a course for seniors who needed an English course for graduation requirements.

On top of knowing nothing about journalism, it was also the course that produced a weekly school paper, which was distributed in the local newspaper, for all to see and critique. There was no extra stipend for this responsibility, and it was more work than any other course in the department.

But here's why teaching can be great- I loved teaching journalism. It was constantly stimulating, I had complete latitude in the curriculum, and the successes of my students were publicly visible, so that my competence as an instructor was not subject to adolescent whims or subjective administrative analysis.

I taught journalism for three years, and stopped because I was officially back in the science department, and the journalism had drained me.

Finding a pace that would leave me standing, not crawling, at the end of the school year sometimes eluded me. My nature, as a young teacher, was to see free time as an opportunity to start a new project. If there were committees to volunteer for that addressed something I believed in, I was always there.

The problem with that is that organizations, at least in my experience at Masconomet, don't worry about putting too much load on an individual.

It is said that the sticky wheel gets the grease.

In my experience, the wheel that can bear the most weight keeps getting most of the burden.

Until it breaks.

When I started teaching, while in the Masters' program at Stanford, I was at one of the best high schools in the Bay Area. The two chemistry classes I taught were filled with excellent students, mature juniors who expected to go to good colleges. I never had any students who were identified discipline problems, nor did I have any students with identified learning issues.

Being only five years older than they were, I had them call me by my first name, and it was never an issue.

The odds of being in a similar teaching situation, for a beginning teacher, parallel those of rich men entering heaven.[18]

When I took my first (very) full-time job back in Massachusetts, I had the good fortune to discuss the issue of how students should address me with an excellent veteran teacher before my

---

[18] Thinking of you here, Trump and Madoff.

first day.   Bill Spencer explained that the Masconomet[19] culture wouldn't support such familiarity, and he was absolutely correct.

As a teacher, you can be friendly with students, but you are not their friend. You have, or ought to seek, an upper hand in the relationship that has often been categorized as "in loco parentis". You'd like to have as much leverage over them as their parents, and, all-too-often, you'll wish you had more.[20]

The second principal in my career really wanted kids to like him. The classic example of this occurred as he stood in front of a group of soon-to-graduate seniors. A colleague watched as he tried to rein in an auditorium growing increasingly out of control.

As he stood at a lectern, a student contemptuously threw a paper airplane on stage. My colleague watched puzzlement pass over the principal's face, and then he picked up the airplane and playfully threw it back into the audience.

The audience roared its approval. The two students sitting in front of her called out "One of us, Steve!" And then one student turned to the other and said, "What an asshole!"

---

[19] The school took its' name from a Native American chief who always honored his treaties. I wonder how that worked out for him.

[20] Because the parents have bargained away leverage. Never negotiate with terrorists.

Although I heard it less toward the end of my career, I always heard from students who wanted extra credit.

This seemed like a fundamentally bad idea, in that it had the potential to draw students away from the goals. However, if you had a student who didn't test well, despite your best efforts, it might be a way to provide some alternative assessment.

If they had just underperformed on a test on balancing equations, I could give them more equations to balance, from another text's teacher's edition, so I wouldn't have to work out the answers myself. The key here was to minimize the extra work for me. The kids who ask for extra credit rarely consider the extra work it represents for the teacher.

Which was why my frequent response to students in science classes asking for extra credit was "Build a small thermonuclear device and detonate it yourself, by hand, while I watch from a safe distance."

I probably should have just said "No".

I did use extra credit for subversive purposes when I was at Woodside. Woodside is very wealthy. The elementary school has a foundation started by parents in 1983 to offset budget cuts. That foundation delivers around two million dollars a year to a school of less than 500.[21]

When kids persisted that year in asking for extra credit, I suggested that I would accept book reports on any of a number of books that had profoundly affected me when growing up. The list included The Autobiography of Malcolm X, Black Boy, Invisible Man, and When the Legends Die.

George Hoberg read at least a couple of those books when he was a sophomore in my class at Woodside. He later told me that they profoundly altered his view of life.

I'm glad it did. Maybe that was the best reason ever to allow extra credit.

———————————————————

At some point, I started using former students to communicate routines and expectations. The way I would do this was to ask students at midyear to write a note to themselves, going back in time to September. They should tell themselves what they needed to know about me, and the class, and expectations. I would explain that I would take these notes, edit them, and hand them out to my next set of students in that class, with their names attached.

I suspect the comments conveyed expectations with more effectiveness than my remarks on opening day. I was always amazed at how students' comments emphasized being on time

[21] The New Yorker, May 27,2013, "Change the World", page 44

and doing homework. What amazed me was the possibility that these were not the expectations in every class.

One student's comments have stayed with me, decades after he was killed in a car crash in his senior year. Marcus was in a low level science class, with lots of special education plans and behavioral issues among his classmates. For years to follow students read the edited version of what Marcus said:

"If you treat him with respect, and your classmates with respect, he will treat you with respect. If you act like an a……………, he'll treat you like an a……………."

Best evaluation I ever got.

Poets, philosophers, and scientists have long commented on the relationship between truth and beauty. My vision of atomic theory was beautiful to me, and I hoped that my students would find beauty that worked for them.

Laurie was a chemistry student of mine who would return to Masco to be a great art teacher. She wrote a piece in the town paper about being in my class. While she wasn't certain what concept she wrote about in the piece, I think it may have been atomic theory. In any case, she articulated well my goals in teaching, both in chemistry and for any subject:

"Unable to understand, I asked my teacher to clarify a particular point.

"As always, he explained it in as many different manners as he knew, to help me see the picture.

"After a pause, something in my brain clicked into place. Suddenly, I knew just what he was talking about, what yesterday's lesson had involved, and how everything else we had learned fit together.

"With the long-needed guidance of this teacher, I began to appreciate chemistry as I would a poem or a painting.

"The point here deals with my teacher serving as a catalyst for my insights. The respect of a teacher for the students' ability to learn is central to helping the students persevere."

Many of the years I taught, I would start the day at 4AM with an hour or more of weightlifting. On one particular day fairly early in my career I arrived at school to find I had to cover a homeroom for another teacher. I normally started my day in this teacher's room for first period, so I was aware that he didn't run a particularly tight ship. I was particularly aware of one diminutive special needs student who would flutter around doing whatever he wished.

I was pretty jacked up after the workout, so I decided the homeroom was going to run right, if only for this one time. I worked at getting students into their seats quickly after the bell rang, since they were supposed to be seated and attentive during announcements.

Everyone was seated- except that one little twerp, who stood twitching behind his chair. Standing on the other side of the lab bench from him in the front of the room, I asked him to sit down.

He ignored me.

I repeated my request, changing it into a directive.

He remained standing, behind his chair, not making eye contact with me. I could see the other students watching the confrontation develop.

I ordered him again to sit down.

When he again ignored me, I vaulted <u>over</u> the lab bench, landing directly behind him. (Stuck the landing, too.)

Did I mention that I was jacked up?

Placing my hands on his shoulders, I forced him down into his seat.

And, as you might expect, he leapt up and attacked me.

Which was fairly comical, given an enormous size differential.

Realizing my stupidity, I backed off, and talked him into walking down to the assistant principal's office.

Discipline is an area where good relations with colleagues can really help you. This incident came at a time when I was in relatively good favor, so I never heard anything about being so stupid as to put my hands on a kid.

Well, actually, I did hear something. Within a fairly short time, the little jerk was in front of the superintendent for a hearing to expel him. When the superintendent listed his attacking me as one of the charges, the kid responded, "That guy jumped over a lab bench to get me. He was crazy!"

The superintendent just laughed. In future years, he would have used that incident to fire me. But, by that time, some sort of statute of limitations had expired, so he had to find fresher material.

By the way, the kid's analysis of my behavior was absolutely correct.

Chapter 3

Getting a Bigger Picture

Although it may be apocryphal, the story has often been told of the Minister of Education in France saying that he knew what every classroom in France was doing at any given moment.

It may be that the story is meant to raise the always-reliable boogeyman of socialism. Or it could celebrate the creativity purportedly inspired by American education and supposedly stifled by the Japanese system.

We live in a country where local control is celebrated as homegrown democracy. That is the same local control that celebrated "states' rights" as an avenue to maintain slavery, and then segregation.

Local control says that a community can have schools as good, and as expensive, as they can fund.

Or as bad.

If education is opportunity, there isn't a much better way to assure that the rich will get richer, and the poor will get poorer.

If we are truly all Americans first and foremost, we must share a commonality of goals.

So, while a national curriculum probably can't be enforced ("Thelma, git ma gun!"), it should be created and assessed.

My involvement with national curricula is kind of a "six degrees of separation" story.

A student I had at Woodside, when I was a teaching intern from Stanford, came east to do his graduate work at MIT. George Hoberg and I reconnected then, several years after I had last seen him when he went to Phillips Exeter Summer School, in Exeter, New Hampshire.

Joe Verrengia was a student of mine in chemistry in Massachusetts. A charming and amusing guy, Joe visited us on many occasions in Exeter, even after he had gone off to Columbia to get his degree in journalism. Joe wasn't a great science student, largely because he had become convinced that he was not good in science and math.

But after he started working for the now-defunct Rocky Mountain News in Denver, he saw that he could carve out a niche for himself by writing about science and technology. To bolster his credentials, Joe wanted to go to a program at MIT for journalists.

So I had George scout out who Joe should talk to, and what to say, to get into the program.

Once Joe was at MIT, one of the requirements he had was to set up a seminar on campus. He chose the topic of space-based missile defense systems- the "Star Wars" fantasy that Reagan bought into from H-bomb physicist Edward Teller.

Joe invited me to bring a handful of my best students to MIT for the panel presentation. I brought four students who had the potential to go to MIT, and they heard the panel say that Reagan's fantasy was just that.

My students asked great questions, since I had made sure they were prepared. An MIT professor in the Materials Processing Center, Ron Latanision, was particularly impressed. As director of the lab, he invited me to bring my students in to tour the lab.

So one day, I brought a busload of students to the lab. I brought students the next year also, and got to know Ron Latanision better over the course of time. Ron was interested in public education, and particularly how MIT could support K-12 education. As our friendship grew over Celtics games in Larry Bird's prime, I was flattered that he sought my suggestions about such collaboration.

I wasn't the only educator with whom Ron was connecting. He became a part of a team that put together a program proposed for federal funding to innovate and upgrade math and science curriculum in the Commonwealth.[22]

On a February vacation in the early 1990's, I was at Whistler skiing, trying to recharge from an ongoing battle with my superintendent at the time. My wife called to tell me that an assistant commissioner of education for Massachusetts had called at home for me. Ron Latanision had recommended me to

---

[22] As I write this, I notice that I'm wearing a t-shirt that came from that program. T-shirts two decades old still function just fine.

work as a leader of the program that was about to get submitted for funding,

Would I come in for an interview in the Commissioner's office as soon as possible?

I asked for a copy of the proposal that was being submitted, and it was at home in Exeter when I got back from Whistler.

My initial reaction to working in the State Department of Education was tepid at best. I didn't hold the department in high regard. They didn't seem particularly relevant to my classroom reality: I couldn't even remember meeting anyone from the department since I had begun teaching.

Then I read the proposal.

At least since my time at Harvard in the mid-Eighties, I had been current with the discussion in science education, and education in general. Some of what I read was useless, but there were also some very good ideas percolating out there.

And the proposal looked poised to tap into all of the good ones.

The proposal didn't get funded that first year. It got improved significantly, and got funded in the next year's round.

Unfortunately, the position I had talked with the Commissioner's office about didn't exist in the second proposal. But I was asked to be a chair on a committee to oversee the development of curriculum frameworks in math and science for Massachusetts.

I've always been lucky, in that when things in my life, or my career, weren't going well, something would come along to restore my confidence, or bolster my reputation.

My association with that initiative was an example of that. But more than that, it was a great opportunity. A hard-working teacher can get lost in his own classroom, and his own school. The Massachusetts initiative gave me a chance to see a much bigger picture, and be a part of it.

It may be in the nature of the subjects of math and science that consensus on national curriculum arrived first. Or it may have been because the National Council of Teachers of Mathematics (NCTM) and the National Science Teachers Association (NSTA) were working on defining a national curriculum in their subjects.

Whatever put science and math out ahead of other subjects, their work helped Massachusetts define its' own frameworks in those areas. Once the frameworks were shaped, then we got to work on developing assessment in those areas. I was in a lot of meetings, and the ones I chaired moved along pretty efficiently. Some meetings and workshops moved at a more languid pace.

Still we got to a point where we had developed assessments in math and science, as well as the newly added cousin of technology. When what I had worked on was sent forward for approval, it was rejected as being too difficult.

Now these assessments had been developed by classroom practitioners, from schools all over the state, as well as other interested stakeholders with whom we worked.

A Department of Education testing guru would later share with me that he thought there was something like racial bias at work: this was seen as too difficult for inner city kids. In our discussions developing the assessments, we had felt we set challenging but attainable standards. If you tell kids they can do something and that you believe in them, they can usually exceed most expectations. If you set low standards for them, you trap them in low expectations-this was exactly what I saw in my experience with most special educators during my career.

After 5 or 6 years of working on the Massachusetts initiative, I was tired of it. So, when our proposed assessments were rejected, I submitted my letter of resignation to the Commissioner.

There would be other battles to fight.

Chapter 4

Masconomet Comes Into Focus

At the beginning of my time served at Masconomet, every teacher would make up their own midterms and final exams. Wisely, Masco came around to having all the teachers for a particular class give the same midterms and finals.

For the supervisors, this would allow them to use actual data to compare teachers.

For me, this would provide data to support my contention that I was as good, if not clearly better, than my colleagues. Being naturally competitive, those exams became one of my major objectives.

After my initially wiping out the other teachers on midyears and finals, one of them started doing significantly better, with his students generally scoring about the same as mine, even in semesters when he had been absent a great deal.

Having common standards and assessment has the potential to force teachers to improve their classroom performance. Without such quantitative measures, a teacher can envelope themselves in a protective cocoon, such as the term "good old boys" implies.

Lee[23] was a good teacher, albeit a difficult colleague. He was bright and hard-working, an enthusiastic performer in the classroom.

His involvement and competence with athletics helped endear him with the principal, who, like Lee, was a local boy who had gone to Salem State.

Lee was odd in some ways as a practitioner. He was extremely possessive of the equipment in his room, which he guarded like a mongoose whose lair adjoined a snake farm. When I began teaching with him, there was a new text in chemistry, which he had apparently chosen. The text was woefully lacking, so I asked him why he had chosen it. His response was "The text doesn't matter."

I couldn't have disagreed more, as I had found the text I used as an intern in California vastly easier for both me and my students. I would be active in future text selections. Years later, while I was at Harvard, I submitted writing samples to a

---

[23] Lee was a baseball coach and football official. He was really tight with Richards, the principal. Richards was a jock-sniffer par excellence, and had even been a cheerleader at Salem State.

When Richards was getting near the end of his time at Masco, he became really big on educational technology. Simultaneously, Lee started getting summer training in computer stuff. When I returned from MIT, Lee was out of the classroom and installed as the superintendent's assistant for technology.

textbook company when they requested it. I also served as a reviewer for a good text that I later recommended we adopt.

Lee was adamantly opposed to the adoption of the text I had reviewed, which just happened to have my name in it.

Suddenly, texts did matter, apparently.

Lee was someone who would take a projector out of your room if he needed it. We both used the old CHEMStudy films early on. In fact, Lee used to take a projector and the films home to show his son, who wasn't seeing them in his chemistry class in another town.

When I took my sabbatical, I worked with the CHEMStudy program to create film notes, worksheets and quizzes to use with the films. These were published, and used internationally by the time I returned from my sabbatical.

At that point, Lee stopped using the films, saying they were outdated.

Apparently hydrogen no longer had just one proton.

At one point, Lee was telling everyone that he was big on "enrichment" in chemistry. That was a cutting edge idea at the time. Texts were working to show students how chemistry was relevant to their lives, and show them diverse role models in science.

So, when we selected a text that was filled with enrichment, I started the year by getting agreement that we would test on the enrichment material on the midyear and finals. Every test I gave that year had items that were intended to gauge that the students had, at a minimum, read the enrichment material.

As the time of the mid-year approached, Lee balked at including items on enrichment. I was quite insistent, both because that was the agreement and because I had busted my ass emphasizing and assessing the enrichment material.

For once, Dr. Post, the department chair, stood his ground with Lee[24], and the assessment items on enrichment stayed on the midyear.

After they had taken the midyear, my students came to me quite upset. They had found out that Lee had given his students a "study sheet" on enrichment. They felt that they were at a disadvantage, since the grade scale at that time was based on how all students did on the exam.

I went into Lee's room and found the study sheet on his desk. It listed specifically on which pages in the text that students should look at the enrichment material, conveniently in the same order as the material appeared on the test. It listed only the enrichment material that was included on the test.

I brought it to Dr. Post, and asked him to address it, in his role as chair. His solution was that the portion of the exam that

---

[24] Post was not really good about standing up to Lee over anything. Lee would refuse to talk to Post if he wasn't getting his way, which Post admitted to me he hated.

included enrichment was no longer to be a part of the grade scale.

My students were outraged at this solution. However, one of them, whose mother was chair of the school committee, said to his classmates, "Don't worry, my Mom is on this."

I was never aware of any consequences for Lee's actions.

It is not that hard for me to imagine how that would have played out if our roles had been reversed.

Even good teachers, faced with high stakes assessment, are going to feel pressure.

Imagine what that pressure feels like to teachers who are insecure, or less than competent.

And there are such teachers out there.

A beginning teacher buys into whatever schedule comes with the new position. I came to Masconomet with a chemistry major and chemistry certification. All of the five classes I taught in my first year were chemistry, at the college prep and lowest level.

When Mark left for two years and Harry came on board, I stayed in chemistry. My understanding and ability to teach the subject grew with each year.

When Mark returned from two years away, at the same time that enrollment was declining, a log jam began. Teaching assignments became a more contentious issue. One would think that adult professionals could sit down together, look at what needed to be taught, and find an equitable distribution.

There were two barriers to that happening. First was Lee, who saw his needs as first priority, and everyone else's as irrelevant.[25]

Second was the power that scheduling held for principals and department heads. If accumulating or exercising power was important, scheduling was a great way to do it.

Notice that, in this exercise, what was best for kids, or teachers, is not a consideration.

When there were extra sections of physics that needed to be taught, Harry picked them up. He may have been certified, for all I know. I suspect his college coursework in physics may have exceeded the two introductory semesters of the subject I had.[26]

Harry worked with the person who had been the "physics department" by himself for years. Bob was an imaginative teacher. Before it was commonplace, he was demonstrating pendulum motion by swinging from a rope in the auditorium,

---

[25] Was Lee raised an only child? A spoiled child? Or did he just cross species and become a jackass?

[26] I took those to meet the requirements for the chemistry major. I guess I could have taken more, but I think I wanted to marshal my resources for the calculus requirement.

doing labs with matchbox cars on velocity and acceleration, and generally making the subject more interesting than it had ever been in my experience.

At some point, Bob had a corridor confrontation with a student whose bad reputation preceded him. I never knew the specifics of it, but it dragged out for a long time. Bob felt that the administration was not supportive, and although it all eventually went away, so did a frustrated Bob. He took his act to a top private school in Washington D.C. There he won national recognition for teaching excellence soon after his arrival.[27]

When Bob was gone, Harry became the physics department. And since there was still one more section than he could teach, I was asked to teach physics.

Now, at this point, I was feeling pretty good about my mastery of chemistry. The insecurity about the subject that was a reflection of poor understanding was gone.

The memories of that insecurity were not gone, however. So, taking on a new subject for which I was poorly prepared was not really appealing. However, John assured me that he could guide me through it, and it would be his chance to pay me back for the help I had provided him.

---

[27] I announced this at a school committee meeting. I thought it was worth the members knowing that a great teacher had been allowed to get away.
The superintendent did not look pleased about this.

And I think that, if I wanted a full-time job, Masconomet wasn't offering any other options.

So I did it for a year. Harry was a great help, doing large group lectures once a week and taking the time to explain what I needed to know to work in the class.

It still was phenomenally stressful, going in each day and hoping my inadequacies weren't going to be exposed.

Of course, they were going to be exposed. The seniors in the class knew me as a chemistry teacher, and saw Harry's guiding hand in what I did.

There was a class in the English department called Rhetoric. In it students wrote often, about whatever they chose, and read their work aloud in class. I was particularly chagrined when a student told me that one of my physics students had written a paper about having me as a physics teacher. She lamented how unfair it was to have physics with a person who clearly wasn't the regular physics teacher, and not doing as good a job at it.

I still remember how mortified I was, since I was doing my best, in a subject I hadn't wanted to teach anyway.

That is my strongest memory from one year of teaching physics.

However, I do have another memory about physics.

After my year in the physics classroom, I could see that there was a need for physics teachers, and I suspected Harry was going to leave Masconomet one way or another, and probably soon.

Boston College saw the need for physics teachers, and created a program to address the need. It would meet on Friday afternoons and weekends, and by the end of a year, you would have physics certification.

I applied and was accepted. So I went to Dr. Brown, who was now superintendent, and asked for a schedule to allow me to be in the program. I don't think I even asked for the district to pay for it, I just needed Friday afternoons.

Dr. Brown turned me down, saying the district couldn't have me missing those Friday afternoon classes.

Several ironies would follow. As it happened, the schedule I got for the next year ended up with my finishing teaching at noon each day. I could have done the program anyway.

The hours on Judy's job were different that next year also. She, too, was free at noon Fridays. So, we were able to leave on our weekends at noon each Friday.

Thanks, Dr. Brown.

Then the time came when Harry was actually going to leave. The district was in a panic about who would teach physics. So, now, Dr. Brown came to me and offered to pay for coursework, at night, over a couple of years, to get certified in physics.

Sorry, Dr. Brown, that train already left the station.

By that point, Dr. Brown may have grown used to my turning him down. The other time he came to me was to teach in his Copernican Plan/Renaissance Program, and he said he really needed my help. At that point, the fiscal constraints he was under made it necessary to find a teacher who could teach Social Studies[28], English, Science, and Math to a small and diverse group of students who would stay with him for most of the day. He said that I was the only person he could see who could begin to do that.[29]

At that point, I was about to apply for the sabbatical that I would actually get, and I had begun working on the CHEMStudy materials that would end up the basis for the sabbatical.

Turning him down that time was particularly satisfying. That was before the Great War, and may have been one more reason he went after me when I returned from the sabbatical.

He was just going to have to make his program work without me.

---

[28] Which I was certified in.

[29] Perhaps Masco's having me teach many different subjects was part of a brilliant plan, whereby they foresaw they would one day need a teacher of such diverse experience.
Or, maybe they were just jerking me around.

Chapter 5

Humoring the Hordes

Research into what students value in a teacher always places a sense of humor high on the list. If you don't have a sense of humor, you better have some other pretty good coping skills in place.

First, it probably is crucial to have the ability to laugh at yourself. For all of the time a teacher spends talking in front of a class, some things will occasionally come out that will be inherently funny, however unintentionally.

When I was teaching a journalism class, I once heard myself say, "The Salem Evening News- that comes out in the morning, right?"

Another time, I heard myself asking students the question, "What river is under the Mystic River Bridge?"

Each time, students roared in laughter at me. I laughed along with them. If they don't see you modeling being comfortable with yourself, it is going to be harder for them to be comfortable with you. Furthermore, students can be more comfortable with themselves if you model it for them.

As my career proceeded, my hairline receded. Students took some pleasure in pointing this out to me. Personally, I feel I have salt and pepper hair with flesh-tone highlights, but students tended to see this as baldness.

When a colleague of mine told students about a day which I don't celebrate- my birthday- students got me an attractive tie. I told them that it was a great looking tie, and I liked the eagle on it.

At which point they felt compelled to point out that it was a bald eagle.

Students who were wiseguys (and gals?) often recognized a kindred spirit in me. I had one student whose routine was to lament at length how every aspect of the universe was conspiring against her. She once labeled and assignment that displeased her as "heinous", which I thought showed great vocabulary skills.[30] Her ongoing whine led one of her classmates to label her as "Princess Positive."

The Princess's venom could be pretty potent, which was part of her act, and she was not above directing it at me. Once, after a particularly sarcastic comment from her, I commented that I thought she had been crushed under Dorothy's house in the tornado.

She did get me back for that, however. In some demonstration in front of her chemistry class, I needed to cool something down, or demonstrate something involving dry ice. I grabbed the classroom fire extinguisher and discharged it in front of the class.

---

[30] I did ask her to verify that there was an "h" at the beginning of the word.

After some of the contents had escaped, I was reminded by their appearance that it was a chemical fire extinguisher- I was in a chemistry room.

Duh.

I was surrounded by this billowing cloud of yellow powder. It settled on me and the lab bench, and the desks in the front row, as students raced away from me and toward the window in back.

After some cleanup, students returned to their desks, as I brushed yellow powder off my clothes.

Laughing at my own stupidity, I asked, "Did I get any in my hair?"

Princess Positive responded, "Why don't you take it off and shake it to find out?"

I loved having her in my class.

In using my own sense of humor in class, I ran the risk that something might be misunderstood, or misheard, or misinterpreted.

One example involved a student named Kerry. Kerry was less than razor sharp, and other students would tease her about it. That was not something I would do, although I once did it inadvertently.

Kerry was standing in front of my desk, talking with other students about the book they had in their English class. Other students took turns complaining about how worried they were about the upcoming test on the book, in view of the fact that they hated the book.

Kerry piped up with the fact that she was going to do just fine. She had, apparently for the first time, discovered Cliff Notes. She felt this meant she would not need to read the book, and would still do great on the test.

I saw a chance to make a joke, although I wasn't directing it at her. However, I didn't think much about her possible reaction, either.

Joining the discussion, I spoke in my most earnest tones, which my wife long ago learned indicated that I was far from serious.

"Kerry," I said. "The problem with the Cliff Notes is that, in being so much shorter than the book, a great deal gets left out or condensed."

"For example, you know how, in The Scarlet Letter, Hester is forced to wear that capital A on her chest?"

"Yes!" Kerry replied, rather eager to show off her newfound knowledge.

"Well," I continued, "in the Cliff Notes, it's a lower case a."

Fully credulous, Kerry responded, "Really?"

Her classmates doubled over in laughter at her. And she turned at looked furiously at me, sure I had been trying to make her look like a fool in front of her peers.

I really wasn't. I kinda wish I could take that one back.

Does make for a pretty good story though.

I shall always remember preparing one particular class to do a titration lab.

One memorable girl was, to use a word that probably goes back to, at least, Mae West, "statuesque".

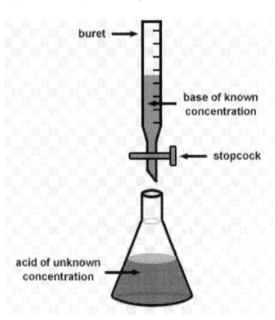

But, far beyond her appearance, she was a joy to be around.

A key part of her charm was that she seemed completely oblivious to her most obvious attributes. She was an enthusiastic member of the cheerleading squad. Yet she never seemed to notice that when she bounded onto the basketball court before a game, the layup line for visiting teams would be disrupted as the adolescent boys stared, temporarily transfixed.

She was the kind of girl I would have wanted to raise. Her naïve innocence seemed of another time, and would be a comfort to any father. Otherwise, you would have to lock her in a convent at age 11 and not release her for a decade.

I was showing her class how titration is done. In her eager enthusiasm, she sat in the front row, as I showed how to manipulate the tall glass burets that would dispense the acid and base. Since everyone would be using a lot of acid and base, there were two large plastic containers on the lab bench where I was demonstrating.

Which was why, as I worked the burets, she said loudly, "Could you move the jugs? I can't see."

She then looked around her, puzzled, as every guy in the class collapsed in laughter.

I stood in front of the class, like a deer in the headlights, or George W. Bush in an unscripted press conference. I bit hard on the inside of my cheek, trying to find a pain level to keep a poker face that would allow me to feign ignorance. Eventually, I was able to continue titrating.

It was during her senior year that she came up to me and said, "Hey, I know now what everyone was laughing at when you did that titration last year."

Sooner or later, reality intrudes into childhood.

—————————————————————————————

During a complex film on x-ray crystallography, I passed a slip of paper with a decimal on it to the very bright kid next to me. He looked at me in the darkness, puzzled. I indicated for him to wait a second. Then I stopped the projector at a point where cosines were being used in a calculation.

I asked Ricky, "What is the cosine of 37 degrees?"

He glanced at the paper and confidently replied, ".783".

I turned on the projector, and the class heard the crew-cut say, "The cosine of 37 degrees is .783."

Ricky's friend looked at him in amazement and said "How did you know that?"

To Ricky's credit, he responded disdainfully, "Everyone knows that!"

It was a few days before he confessed the ruse to his friends.[31]

I only taught English fulltime for a year at Masco. I continued teaching journalism for two more years. The success and positive reinforcement I got in that year probably kept me from thinking about leaving Masco for several years.

As a career move, it would have been a good time to leave. I could have left behind institutional memories of any mistakes I made, and brought to a new workplace any wisdom and maturity accumulated in those beginning years.

My dad used to change superintendencies every five years or so. Partly, that was because he was climbing a career ladder to larger communities. But I think it was also that he realized that, in coming to a community as a change agent, he was always building some enemies with every change he made.

He was smart enough to get out of town before antagonism built to a critical mass.

---

[31] I just made those numbers up now. Who knows that crap anyway? Rainman?

Perhaps, because I didn't have his career ambitions, I wasn't so smart.

When I moved into the English department, I got the first supervisor/manager who really seemed to appreciate me. I admired the English department head because he willingly taught sections of the lowest level of students. That made his giving me a lower level course for seniors, which I came to think of as Words on Parade, very acceptable.

Words on Parade was mostly focused on reading and writing skills, with emphasis on adolescent literature. I got my teaching schedule in the spring of my leave of absence, so he gave me the books for the courses I would be teaching.

One of the books for Words on Parade[32] was a classic in adolescent literature called <u>The Chocolate War</u>[33].

In May, I sat poolside next to my mother at her place in Florida, reading the book. I stopped, astonished, and said to her, "Mom, this book has masturbation in it!"

She replied, "Well, you'll just have to be careful, dear."

Thanks, Ma.

The teaching of journalism, as well as two other courses in a new department, kept me moving at an exhausting pace. By

---

[32] I'm tempted to identify this course by its acronym. However, being so highly sensitive to the feelings of others, I will avoid any possibilities of cultural overtones.

[33] <u>The Chocolate War</u>, Robert Cormier

spring, I was exhausted, but still standing, propped up by the positive reinforcement I was getting from the department head. He was probably the person who showed me supplementary materials I could use in class. Because The Chocolate War was in such common usage, there were materials available to give to students. There were essay questions, vocabulary lessons, quizzes, and whole pages of fill-ins to evaluate whether students were doing the reading.

One day, we were going over a sheet of fill-ins in class. I was calling on different students to give their answers, when we got to a question that roused some of the less participatory members of the class.

"Have Bobby read his answer to this one!" more than one of the troupe urged. Bobby was a ringleader in this group, but having him volunteered, even by others, to participate seemed like a real coup to me.

Gratefully, I urged Bobby to go ahead.

Bobby read the opening to the fill-in, "Jimmy was a good football player because………….."

I should have caught the anticipation building in the class, but I missed it.

"………….he had really strong arms from jacking off so much," Bobby read, beaming at his contribution.

Kids fell on the floor howling, as I realized I had forgotten all about that "sensitive" aspect of the book.

I had no idea what to do or say. When a student had a grand mal seizure in this class weeks earlier, I had been prepared, and had dealt with it calmly.

This, I wasn't prepared for.

The roar finally died down, without my having thought of a word to say.

At that point, a painfully shy girl, who would later tell me that she had been molested as a child by an ABC student the family hosted, spoke up.

Her voice, so rarely heard in that class, said "Maybe he was just lonely."

She had thrown me a lifeline.

"Yes," I said. "He was probably lonely. It's perfectly normal[34], now let's move on."

And, thankfully, we did.

———————————————————————

One of the things the department head told me about teaching the lower level kids was that they loved having you read to them. That became a regular feature of Words on Parade. I would read aloud from the book we were working on. Or I

———————————————————————

[34] I don't remember if I meant loneliness was normal, or masturbation was. It didn't matter anyway, to a drowning man.

would bring in something I thought lent itself to oral treatment[35].

When I was a kid, my Dad would read aloud to my sister and me, as his parents had done with him[36] decades earlier. I brought in a well-worn book that my Dad had read to us, My Life and Hard Times , by James Thurber. The kids enjoyed the humor, and it made me feel connected to my Dad, and my own childhood.

Another time, I was reading aloud from a Hemingway short story, "Fathers and Sons", I believe. While the kids listened silently, I became aware of the rhythms of the spoken word in Hemingway's work.

Through word choice, and sentence and paragraph length, Hemingway seemed to be intentionally mimicking the rhythms of foreplay and sex!

I looked around the room, hoping that no one, particularly Bobby, was noticing this. Fortunately, no one did.

That experience was a great insight for me. I'd always liked writing, but had never thought much about the flow of words.

---

[35] Too bad David Sedaris' Santaland Diaries wasn't available as a special treat at Christmastime. On second thought, that might have been disastrous.

[36] "In the slums of Everett, Massachusetts," I can hear him saying.

Hemingway made me a better writer, more conscious of the rhythm of writing[37].

That is a pretty good reason for him to be taught in our schools.

Another English class I taught was about vocabulary and grammar. The vocabulary was there as preparation for the SAT's, and the grammar was there because, well, it was English class.

I gave weekly vocabulary quizzes, to force students to learn the lengthy lists they faced. Teaching vocabulary never intimidated me, as I had always been a reader[38]. I had also, since early childhood, taken the "It Pays to Increase Your Word Power" quizzes that were in the Reader's Digests stocked in all our bathrooms at home.[39]

Teaching grammar wasn't bad, since my parents had been correcting my grammar since I was little. Language always interested me, so elucidating the rules of it with kids was fun.

This course was a college prep level course for seniors, so behavioral issues were much less of a concern than in Words on

---

[37] There are no hidden rhythms, or secret codes, in this book, even though I lived in the same town as Dan Brown.
[38] When I was in elementary school, the Springfield paper published a picture of me leaving the town library with a huge stack of books.
[39] I also read the Digest's humor columns, mining them for dirty jokes. Still looking.

Parade. That made it much less hazardous waters when we sailed into the conjugation of the verbs "to lie" and "to lay".

Students were going over their answers together on fill-ins about using the correct verb form. Karla, a cute, cheerful kid whose dad headed the music department, picked a regrettably quiet moment in the class to check an answer with her partner.

"Did you get 'lied' for that?" she asked.

"Because I got 'laid'," she said within hearing of everyone in class.

I didn't have any comment on that one, but, with those kids, I felt I could laugh along with them.

Karla's dad told me later he thought it was pretty funny himself.

Chapter 6

Journalism- A New Way to Activism and Subversion

Probably because faculty got a copy of the students' weekly contribution to the town papers in their mailboxes[40], my successes in the English department were widely known.

One of my more insecure colleagues came to me and said, "I don't know how you could just move in and teach English so well. I couldn't do that."

Sometimes the siren call of a great joke obscures any need, or ability, to think about the impact of the joke on the listener.

My faux humble response was probably the last thing I should have said to that insecure individual:

"It's not that hard. It is my native language."

Actually, because teaching is so language-dependent, I think many more teachers should have the experience I had teaching English. It made me more critical as I looked at students' written work when I returned to science. Students would protest that English shouldn't matter in science class, but I

---

[40] That was my idea. The school only had two subscriptions to the local paper, so most teachers wouldn't see it. Administrators were doing little to keep faculty informed, so I took it upon myself. That wasn't altruism, but more like taunting- "See what I can do!"

would point out that science still required effective communication.

Teachers have a lot to deal with in schools, but they should be effective communicators, in both speech and writing.

If we are teaching subjects in English, even when it is a second language for the students, shouldn't we be fluent enough in English to teach it as a subject?

It is, after all, our native language in the United States.

_____

One of my first steps in teaching journalism was getting a staff of students organized, and getting them to buy into responsibility.

My first journalism class came in having signed up for the course before I had received the teaching assignment. After that first class, I did some recruiting to get a few key students in the course. Ironically, our greatest successes, in terms of winning awards, came with that first class.

I asked for students to apply for the job of editor in chief. Then I interviewed each candidate, looking for energy and commitment. I ended up choosing Lisa, a student I had previously taught in science, and whose family I had known since I taught her older brother.

Lisa and I then asked for applications from within the class for each of the other editorial positions. We interviewed the candidates, and I let Lisa make the final decisions, so she would have a commitment to her staff.

The most important position to fill may have been sports editor. With all the different sports, and different levels of each sport, we were going to try to get all of that reporting done by volunteers outside the class. That meant the sports editor would need to ride herd on people who weren't in the class, and over whom we had no leverage. She also could go to individual coaches to try to get them to find a reporter, if no volunteers came forward.

I knew that there were probably going to be more eyes total on the sports coverage than everything else we did. However, I really didn't care that much about it. The bar set by the previous work in the town paper was at a level a slug could crawl over. I wanted to use our class resources for things that interested me, and on which I could get my students to commit.

I explained to the students in the class that working on the paper was going to be just like the real world. There were going to be plenty of stories that we would have little enthusiasm for, but which would still have to be done. Stories about the prom, and graduation, and the school play were expected every year and would have to be done, however tedious.

But we also would brainstorm for ideas each week. If someone had a great idea, they could own it, and do the story. I also contributed ideas, and, if I could sell them, we would find someone to cover them.

So I spent the next three years with my eyes open, looking for stories and ideas that interested me, or seemed truly important.

Although I think I taught the students about the W's and the H of stories[41], we would take major stories and discuss logical questions the reporter should be asking. Once our first edition was published, we would go over the articles that had been published each week and analyze what questions had gone unasked. After a few weeks, kids in the class had a pretty solid idea of what they were doing.

From the time I got the assignment to teach the class, I was thinking of people who would be interesting to interview. The first few interviews we did of people who were the focus of an article were done in class, so students would get the sense of how to interview.

In the spring before I started teaching journalism, I was at an annual high school basketball tournament called the Boston Shootout. I spotted a reporter for the Boston Globe whose work I had long admired, Bob Ryan. Bob had covered the Celtics practically since his first days after leaving Boston College. His writing was insightful, and filled with political, social and historical references that were completely atypical of

---

[41] I had no text for the course when I began, which was somewhat freeing. Since we had a paper to get out weekly, finding time to use a text would have been problematic. By the way, I think it was Who, What, Where, When, Why, and How.

sports writing[42]. The Globe sports section was generally viewed as the best in the country, and Bob was one of its leading stars[43].

So I walked up to Bob, introduced myself, and told him that I was about to begin teaching journalism[44].

Bob was the friendly and personable guy one sees so often now on ESPN, so I asked him if he would come to my class to talk about writing. He agreed to come, once I got started in the fall.

---

[42] Bob would say this was due to "good Jesuit education."

[43] Ryan would write numerous books, including working with Larry Bird on his autobiography, Drive! He would win the national Sportswriter of the Year award many times.

[44] By the time I got to UNH, I had eliminated any fear of meeting new people, no matter how intimidating they might seem. When I walked up to some great-looking female and began talking to her, I would have guys who had never left their New Hampshire farms say, "How can you talk to her?"

I'd respond, "Did you see her? How can you not talk to her?"

So Bob was our first big class interview. I picked a writer who I had established to have good skills, and who was really enthusiastic about the opportunity. Then we interviewed Bob as a class, and the reporter and I continued to interview him for another hour afterwards. Bob is colorful, direct, opinionated, and very smart, so we just needed to ask good questions.

The student wrote up the interview, with my making suggestions for revisions several times. It was nice that there was no fixed deadline for the story, so we could rework it to our final satisfaction.

In the spring, that interview won the national award as the best high school sports-writing of the year. It was the nature of Bob Ryan himself that guaranteed it would be a good story, but that was a nice way to start out my experience teaching journalism.

I've always been reluctant to fail students, since a D- isn't going to get them much further than an F. However, in teaching journalism and putting out a weekly paper, we were engaging in a real world experience[45]. Since people get fired in the real world, I should have failed kids in journalism, two in particular.

One of them was the first photo editor we had. Lisa had picked her because she was a friend, but she really thought she could

---

[45] Which would be verified by calls from readers, like the one saying our coverage of a daughter's junior varsity softball team was woefully inadequate. I explained that we were using the best volunteer writers we could. I didn't say that I didn't really give a shit.

get her to do the job. Boy, was she wrong. We got week after week of excuses for the absence of photos. The paper looked like "The Old Gray Lady" that was the print-heavy New York Times.

I think we got one picture out of Sally, all semester. <u>One.</u>

I should have failed her. Sally was planning on becoming a nurse, and a failure to meet responsibilities there could be a lot more costly. I failed to give her that lesson at a time when the cost would be minimal.

The other journalism student I should have failed was one who produced exactly one article all semester. He also had many excuses for his lack of productivity. The one article he did write was just an editorial on how classy Celtics fans were. That required no research, no interviews, just an opinion he thought was worthy- his own.

His father came to me when I announced I would be failing his son and talked me out of it. I never should have listened. The son went on to the University of Miami, where he flunked out. The father came back to me afterwards, and said I had been right, I should have flunked his son. It would have been a lot cheaper than the University of Miami.

_____

Another idea that caught my attention that first year was the four day school week. I read about a couple of districts in New England that had started such a schedule. As someone enamored of three day weekends, it sounded like heaven to me.

Furthermore, it made a certain amount of sense for Masco. Geographically, it was a big district, with students at the outskirts spending a long time on the bus getting to school. If we made the day longer, they could spend one day less riding the bus[46]. The fifth day could be for athletic competitions, or other extra-curricular activities. The potential for savings on busing costs and school heating bills, at a time when I'd been laid off from science due to a tight budget, might justify the change.

Because this was strictly my idea, I decided to forgo pitching it in the weekly brainstorming. Instead, I thought it would seem more important to the writers on it if we lent it an air of Woodward and Bernstein. So I picked two writers, both named Gregg, and Lisa and I asked them if they wanted to work on this secret project. They could discuss it with no one except us and their parents.

They would need their parents' co-operation in a bit of subterfuge. Their parents would have to write them excuses to get out of school for a day, so they could go visit a district in Maine where the 4 day week was in place.

The parents agreed. The boys went to the district, and interviewed people there. Then they calculated potential

---

[46] It also would have meant for longer class blocks, which we were proposing before Dr. Brown came up with his Copernican Plan.

savings for the district, misleading Dr. Brown about why they were asking him for busing and heating costs.

When the article came out, no one had seen it or heard of it, except the reporters, Lisa, and me. It generated a lot of buzz in the school. To my amusement, the head of the music department stood up in a faculty meeting and asked when Masco would be going to a four day week.

As far as I know, the idea never received serious consideration at any level in the district.

But we entered it into the Globe's annual competition for high school newspapers in Massachusetts. There were four categories in which prizes were given. It won the first place award in the features category[47].

As far as I know, Dr. Brown's Copernican Plan never won any awards.

_____

I had another idea for a story that first semester. Again, it promoted an agenda of my own[48].

Masco's football program was pretty poor. To my analysis, the cause was the head coach. Phil was a former Marine Lieutenant Colonel, who ran the program with all the inflexibility one would

_____

[47] Despite the total absence of pictures. We came up with graphs of potential savings, and charts of a proposed longer school day.
[48] I hear you saying "What a surprise! How totally out of character!"

have predicted. For the community, at that time, his coaching was anachronistic.

In contrast, the soccer program won the league title year after year. The coach was a young math teacher, the only member of his department who showed imagination and relevance in teaching the subject. Lenny had been an All-American in soccer at BU, and would run and scrimmage with his kids.

The premise of the article was whether Masco could support both a football and a soccer program. We did graphs, again in the absence of photos, showing the imbalance in the historical success of the programs. The writer interviewed people connected with both programs, including past football coaches. I was hoping there would be criticism that would highlight what I saw as the current shortcomings. Unfortunately, no one seemed willing to come forth with opinions as strong as I'd hoped.

The football coach ended up coaching the team for a couple more years before he was replaced. After he left, the football program went through one or two head coaches, and then settled on my friend Jim, who ran the program for kids who didn't fit in well with traditional classes at Masco. Jim has been enormously successful with the program.

The soccer program continued to be successful year after year under the young math teacher.

Masco could support both football and soccer.

Of course, I kinda knew that all along.

Gregg's story won first place in sports in the Boston Globe contest, giving us two of the four statewide firsts that year. Ironically, the Bob Ryan interview won nothing in the Globe competition that year. That may indicate the subjectivity of such awards. Or it may just be that the judges thought that giving an award to an article interviewing a Globe sportswriter might seem a little self-serving.

When the Globe awards were announced, I excitedly called the editor of the local paper. She made it the top story on the front page.

Public validation is very gratifying.

Other ideas I came up with didn't win awards, but either amused me or promoted another agenda of mine.

We did an article that purported to evaluate student awareness of the world around them. Students were asked to identify the names of people in a photo array. As I had hoped, vastly more students were able to identify Mikhail Gorbachev than the superintendent, whose office was 30 yards from the school but was rarely seen in the corridors. The headline I chose was "Provincial or Cosmopolitan?" Hopefully, that didn't obfuscate the point I was trying to make.

In another survey, students were asked to name their favorite teachers, by department and for the whole school. At that point, there was no formalized way of gathering students assessment of their teachers; that would be years in coming. I had been doing it since I began teaching, and I knew that other teachers I respected did also. I wanted to make the point that it was disrespectful not to include students input.

I was astonished when students named every teacher in the school except one. I had thought that there would be numerous teachers who would be shut out. We said in the article that there had only been one teacher who got no votes, but we did not identify her. She continued teaching for years afterwards, until she eventually calcified and was wheeled off to retirement.

Another idea I had which won a prize with my second group of students involved a place I'd driven by for years that always creeped me out. The Danvers State Mental Hospital was no more than five miles down the interstate from the school, and it entirely looked the part. Its Gothic exterior seemed to promise all sorts of horrors inside, and, in fact, would serve as a filming location for a horror movie some years later.

Chris was a recruit in my second class who would become editor. She was bright, vivacious, and an excellent writer. So she went to the hospital for a tour, equipped with her camera. Her story answered the questions people had about the mysterious place, and her photos showed the darkened and gloomy corridors of the facility.

I wrote great college recommendations for Chris, and was irate when Stanford turned her down. I called the admissions office to let them know how disappointed I was, and was amazed when the Dean of Admissions called me back at my home. He explained how competitive the process was, and how they undoubtedly turned down students who would have been fine at Stanford.

I guess it might have been because I was an alumnus, but his call made me feel like someone had treated me with the respect I felt all professionals should deserve.

Chris went to Michigan, loved it, and went on to law school.

———————————————————————

Another of my agenda-driven story ideas that won a prize from the Globe involved South Boston High School. Early in my career, the court-ordered integration of the Boston Public Schools had been headlined around the world. South Boston High School had been ground zero for that cultural confrontation[49].

It was some years later when I began teaching journalism, and I wondered how things had changed at South Boston High School. The principal, Jerry Winegar, had been brought in by court order at the height of the busing conflagration. Winegar had been a principal in St. Paul just before he took the South

---

[49] Common Ground, by Anthony Lucas, is a Pulitzer Prize-winning story of those years.

Boston job, so I figured he would know of my dad, even if he hadn't known him.

My idea was to have the students in my journalism class participate in a student exchange with South Boston. I knew how sheltered I had been from urban realities at Highland Park, and I thought suburban Masco students were even more sheltered and unaware. And, even though I was critical of Masco's shortcomings, I wanted them to see how fortunate they were by comparison, and the opportunity that surrounded them.[50]

We arranged for families to participate on each end, with students staying overnight with host families. I drove students in to Southie in the school van on the day the exchange began. I sat in on classes, and was saddened to see the state of education there. I saw a chemistry class where they worked on a lab on density. This was a lab that my students might have done in the beginning of the year, or might just as well have done as freshman. The Southie students were doing this in the spring. One student spent the whole lab wandering about, claiming someone had hidden his jacket. The teacher never made any significant effort to get him to get back in the lab.

In contrast, I went to a Social Studies class, where they had a guest speaker. He actually was more of a guest interviewer. Jonathan Kozol, whose first book I had read while at Stanford, was interviewing students for a project he was working on. I

---

[50] I did worry that the exchange would make the Southie student resentful, but that didn't seem to occur.

was so impressed to find someone like him at Southie. Winegar told me that the notoriety of the school made it easy to get involvement of committed liberals, whether personally or through financial contributions.

I left my kids at the school, to stay overnight in Southie and Dorchester. The Southie kids came out to Masco the next day. I had contacted all the Boston TV stations about the exchange. The only one that chose to provide coverage was the PBS station, which sent a camera crew to film the story. I had warned my kids to be careful about what they said on camera. When Chris realized he had been asked a question meant to make the education at Southie look bad, he intentionally stammered and responded in a manner that rendered the question unusable.

On a follow up, students went into Boston, on what happened to be St. Patrick's Day, to interview principals from the busing story. Tiffany came back shaken by the depth of emotion of one of the busing opponents, Pixie Palladino, who cried at having her kids' neighborhood school taken away. Although Tiffany saw Pixie's opposition to busing as largely based in prejudice, the depth of her feeling registered deeply.

Jennifer, who had become the first highly committed and competent photo editor, went to the St. Pat's Day breakfast in Southie. A highly political event organized by Whitey Bulger's politician brother Billy, it drew all the movers and shakers in Boston. Jennifer met the flamboyant (and racist) long-time City Councilman Albert "Dapper" O'Neill. Dapper proceeded to squire her around, introducing her to all the big names like she was his daughter[51]. She invited him to come to Masco for a class interview. He accepted, but not without putting a scare into her by telling her that he carried a gun wherever he went.

My kids got material for essays on their college applications, as well as a great story. We won another prize from the Boston Globe. And maybe a few kids' lives were changed, at least for a while.

In our first year, a Masco grad got national attention when she did well in the U.S. Tennis Open. This came at the same time that a major star, Martina Navritalova, I think, revealed that she was a lesbian.[52] Along with that came rumors of other lesbians on the tennis circuit.

So we sent our sports editor to interview Masco's tennis star. Although she squirmed at asking it, she inquired about lesbianism on the circuit. The Masco grad said she wasn't really aware of it.

Three decades later, that woman would reveal, through the Boston Globe and other media outlets, that she had been sexually abused by her male tennis coach at the time, and how it had harmed her life forever.

---

[51] Dapper lived all his life with his mother. Jennifer was probably not his only surrogate child.

[52] It is nice that, three decades later, we seem to be moving toward a time when such a revelation's newsworthiness would seem quaint.

So she had good reason if she found the question about lesbianism in women's tennis ironic.

The successes of our first year opened doors for us. The Lawrence Eagle Tribune decided to sponsor an annual conference for high school journalists, and asked me to be the first keynote speaker. I took a handful of students and we spent the day at the paper. Dr. Brown was put in the position of offering words of praise for me that could be used by the Eagle staffer who introduced me.[53] He described me as being like Don Quixote, tilting at windmills. Much later, I would see the plaque friends had given him, calling him Don Quixote[54].

When the luncheon came, I stood at a podium , waiting to be introduced. Just before I was to speak, one of my students put a slip of paper on the podium saying, "Your fly is open."

It wasn't, and the speech was well-received. I used the honorarium to have a printer make letter head for our school paper, with the names of all the editorial staff on it. I'm sure that letterhead made its way into a few college applications.

---

[53] I should have asked for a copy of what he gave them. Dr. Brown, who did have somewhat of a sense of humor, described his words of praise as "creative writing". It would have been great to confront him with those words in the arbitration hearings.

[54] It also turns out that he was an underachieving class clown in high school. Freudians, take your mark!

It may have been that day that we approached the Eagle Tribune about submitting articles covering Masconomet for their publication.

We started running articles in their paper. We also started sending articles to the other papers delivered in the Masconomet area, the Beverly Times and the Salem Evening News. Although I hadn't begun word processing at that point, the kids had, through computer classes. A sharp young guy teaching them computers set it up so we could send stories to the other papers electronically. That seems insignificant in the era of e-mail, but back then, it seemed miraculous.

Sometimes the papers wanted a re-write of what we were putting in the local Tri-Town Transcript, and sometimes they accepted the same material.

The publisher of the Transcript, Bill Wasserman, was notoriously irascible. He sent the message through the editor of the Transcript that they wanted any article we published in the Transcript to be re-written before it was used anyplace else.

Like a franchise chain that expands too fast, I had spread our resources too thin. The visionaries in management at Masco didn't offer any additional resources to help me get the journalism done, so, by the third year, we were sending out fewer articles to the other local papers.

———————————————————————

The success of our first year also got us onto a Sunday morning television show called "The Young Editors". The show brought significant newsmakers in to be interviewed by high school journalists.

We interviewed Kay Fanning, the Pulitzer Prize-winning editor of the Christian Science Monitor. We prepared like crazy for the show. It was our good fortune that one of the students in the journalism class had a dad who wrote for the Monitor. We had him come in, and discussed what would be good questions.

Which was why Fanning was somewhat taken aback when Margaret asked her how the Monitor could report on issues in medicine when Christian Scientists don't use traditional medicine. Thanks to our preparation, that and our other questions were delivered in a professional manner, with clear enunciation, appropriate rate of speech, and good eye contact.[55]

Ironically, Fanning was not the person we were originally scheduled to interview. Barney Frank ended up having to change to another week. We might have made national news. Barney had not been "outed" at that point, but rumors were circulating. I wouldn't have been surprised if my kids had insisted on asking him, on camera, if he was gay.

---

[55] It was just like Sam Donaldson in the White House press conferences, but without Donaldson's suspicious resemblance to Satan.

The second and third year I taught journalism, I was officially back in the science department. Dr. Post chafed a little at my being out of his department for part of the time. In the second year, I still wanted to do the newspaper, and the school wanted me doing it[56].

By the third year, I was running out of ideas, and groomed a young member of the English department to take it over. The superintendent fired him for something inappropriate involving a female student[57].

That spring, I got a call from the publisher, Wasserman. He reamed me out for something he didn't like that we had published.

He didn't even pay my salary, and I had jerks at Masco who were already good at giving me grief.

I was done with journalism at Masco at that point. The school assigned journalism to a member of the English department

---

[56] Dr. Brown even forced Richards, who was his assistant superintendent at that point, to put a telephone in my room for kids to use in journalism. I heard from the AV guy who installed it how much that fried Richards. Richards was zealously guarding what little power Dr. Brown had left him.

[57] Although the teacher was officially dismissed for not actually possessing the needed certification. One would kinda think that the geniuses in administration would have verified that when they hired the guy two years earlier.

who had headed the Renaissance faculty. Dave was not great on deadlines or organization.

He was followed by a Dartmouth grad who had been in Social Studies and Special Education for years. Nick had actually worked in journalism, writing for the Hartford Courant. That didn't work out either.

Not my problem.

When I finally left Masco, journalism had once again been assigned to a beginning teacher.

Chapter 7

That Fancy Prep School

Although I never ended up applying to Harvard, having the Phillips Exeter Summer School on my application was probably why I got admitted to Berkeley for college.[58]

The Exeter experience made me acquiesce to applying there for a post-graduate year after high school. There were no females yet in the regular session, so my application probably still lacked great enthusiasm. Or it could have been the two Academy teachers who I had underwhelmed in Summer School that kept me from being accepted.

While I was at UNH, the Academy started accepting female day students. My younger sister was accepted in the first class. She had been breezing through Peabody High School, getting A's without being really challenged[59]. I saw how hard she worked. Often, I would walk through her bedroom late at night, and she would be asleep sitting up in her bed, the book she had been

---

[58] My dad had taken me around UNH in the fall of my senior year in high school. He showed me his football pictures in the field house, and where he had stood outside my mother's dorm, serenading her. I was sold.
Can you imagine how being at Berkeley in the early Seventies would have changed me?

[59] In contrast to me, she was always the oldest in her class. She always had a determination to get straight A's. That may be a female-linked gene in my family.

reading still in her lap. She also wasn't getting all A's anymore, which was enormously stressful to her.

Although my expectations for myself had been raised by that point, my work ethic and maturity still had the baseline in sight. The regular session of the Academy wouldn't have been for me.

As I began teaching, I was a huge advocate of the Summer School. A student I taught at Woodside, George Hoberg, came east for summer school after my first year of teaching at Masco. He had a great experience, and got admitted to Berkeley after high school[60].

At Masco, I started recommending Phillips Exeter Summer School to students who would benefit from it. The first of my Masco students to go there probably came after I had started teaching Chemistry at the Summer School.

My first summer as a teacher there came at a fortuitous time. I had been laid off from the science department, and took a leave of absence rather than exercise my contractual rights to bump into the English department.

While I could intellectually understand that my being laid off was somewhat a result of diminishing budget and declining enrollment, the experience in applying for merit pay made me take the layoff very personally.

---

[60] That was undoubtedly more of an accomplishment for him as an in-state student than my being admitted from the hinterlands in Minnesota.

I might actually have come to doubt myself, except that now I was teaching at Phillips Exeter.

Early in summer school that year, I had another reminder of Masconomet. There was a part-time position teaching Chemistry at Wellesley High School. It was a long commute, but, being part-time, I figured I could avoid rush hour traffic, and who knew how things might evolve.

I interviewed with their personnel director, who happened to be a former chemistry teacher. The interview went well, and at the end, he asked me to teach him some chemistry. He asked me to explain the relationship between reaction rates and a molecular velocity distribution graph. I had over the first few years in the classroom found a great way to do that, so I was on it, like Mickey Mantle on a pitch down the middle[61].

Impressed, he told me they would just need to get a contract approved by the school board.

As he went out to let the superintendent know he had made a decision, I overheard the conversation between them. The superintendent said to him, "His principal told me that he had seven absences this year[62]."

---

[61] Feel free to make up your own Alex Rodriguez joke here.

[62] I was really pissed off and resentful by the end of that year at Masco. While most other years I used to drag myself in if at all possible, I didn't that spring. And, if that happened on a Friday or Monday, all the better.

Realizing that the door was open, and that I was within earshot, they moved further away, and I didn't hear the rest of what the superintendent might have heard from Richards.

I left the office having been told that a contract from Wellesley would be forthcoming.

It never forthcame.

My father went into Massachusetts General Hospital that summer, with complications from his diabetes. He was there for six months, and left a foot behind. Except when I was doing summer school, I was able to be there almost daily. I helped him when he got out of the hospital, taking him to appointments and helping him learn to walk with a prosthesis.

Through that time, my father came to see me as something more like an equal than just a son. After all my parents had done for me up to that point, it was great being able to help them when they needed it.

If I had gotten the job in Wellesley, doing that would have been much harder, and the stresses in my life vastly higher.

Things always work out for me.

Thanks, Mr. Richards.

As a young teacher, I sought ever more student contact. My wife and I would go to a couple of Masco basketball games a week. I'd play basketball with kids after school. We would have groups of kids up to our house. I applied to be a class advisor, which gave Richards another opportunity to turn me down for something.

Being immersed in the 24/7 life of a boarding school looked like nirvana to me[63]. Academy faculty talked about being "triple threats": being in a classroom, a dorm, and coaching. Summer school would give me a sense of that experience.

We ran a girl's dorm, Hoyt Hall. Our girls adopted the name "Hoyt Hoydens"[64]. We loved our girls, and stayed in a great faculty apartment. (Of course, we also had a house 200 yards away, but we wanted the additional contact.)

Chemistry was great. Students were motivated, and I had double periods every day for six weeks. Although we didn't have much time for lab work, we surveyed a year's worth of chemistry in that time, and students averaged 80th percentile on a national ACS exam[65]. I played basketball with kids in the gym every day, and got to do some informal coaching there.

One of my chemistry students scored at the 99th percentile. David was rather a nerd, but he really took to us. Although unathletic, he started running with Judy. His experience at the Summer School led him to graduate high school early, go to Cornell, and then on to medical school.

---

[63] You can make your own "Smells like Teen Spirit" joke here.

[64] You'll need to look it up- it probably has never been common usage.

[65] I knew that Dr. Brown's long blocks could work at Masco before anyone else, since I'd taught that way.

For six weeks, Exeter seemed the perfect environment.

Early in Dr. Brown's tenure as superintendent, before it became clear that we were natural adversaries, I went to see him one spring with a request for a leave of absence.

Because I didn't yet have reason to distrust him, I explained that the reason was that I had found there was going to be a part-time opening at Phillips Exeter Academy during the regular session for the next year. It was only one class, but they had contacted me, and it seemed like that would be my chance to make inroads to a permanent position there.

Dr. Brown said he would hold the application for a while. He said that until the Academy was certain of class enrollments, I shouldn't count on the position actually occurring.

Then, sometime later in the spring, the academy said that they wouldn't need me, because of the way enrollment in chemistry classes had played out.

I let Dr. Brown know he didn't need to submit the application for a leave.

While he had let a physics teacher get away, I wasn't able to make my escape. Whether Brown's fingerprints were on that, I'll never know.

Another summer we stayed in a dorm that was named Dunnan Hall for the session. This was probably because that might mask the fact that we were staying in the infirmary. We had one other adult who shared duty with us.

Carey was a photography instructor who had come to Exeter with a recommendation from the rival prep school at Andover. He was a complete space shot. He would sit at meals in the dining hall, removing bits of food from his beard- and then eating them.

Being in the infirmary, we had the advantage of common access to a refrigerator on the students' floor. We used to buy popsicles to leave in the freezer, for kids to access on the hot summer nights. Carey thought this was a great place to store his beer. He took exception when I told him that he couldn't do that, since students would also be able to access his beer. In fact, he exploded with anger, and appeared like he would attack me[66].

One week, we left Carey in charge for a Saturday night, so we could retreat to a condo we had in northern New Hampshire. Kids roamed free all night long, and tormented one of the weaker students, who barricaded himself in his room after Carey didn't respond to knocks on his door.

We heard about all of this from the students and infirmary staff when we returned the next day. We saw with our own eyes

---

[66] I told the summer school director that this made Carey seem not merely unbalanced, but also suicidal.

that the CPR doll, Resusci-Annie, had her clothes in a disheveled state.

She may have even been defiled.

The potential downside of being in a dorm was now evident.

After I returned to Masco following a year off, I had started teaching journalism. Because I enjoyed that so much, I asked to teach journalism at the Exeter Summer School. I got one of my most energetic and charismatic students ever in that class. John Bremen even came back one summer to be my teaching intern in journalism[67]. All of the students' work, but John's in particular, was so good that the employees at the town paper, where we had our paper printed weekly, used to set aside copies for themselves because they liked the work.

I also had my first experience with student plagiarism while at the Academy Summer School. Students were writing a preview of the Olympics that was occurring in the summer of 1988. I was particularly proud of the work one students had done in her coverage of some sports. That was until I had another faculty member point out that it had been lifted, largely verbatim, from

---

[67] In the picture that follows, he is the dapper young man in front of David Halberstam.

the New York Times[68]. While she wasn't kicked out, we did go through disciplinary steps and thoroughly frighten her.

While teaching journalism at Phillips Exeter, I got my best guest speaker ever, a man who was a true hero of mine.

David Halberstam won the Pulitzer as a young New York Times reporter in Vietnam. His revelations of what was actually going on there angered Jack Kennedy enough that the President called the Times' publisher and asked him to fire Halberstam- and the publisher refused.

Halberstam later wrote a book about Vietnam, <u>The Best and the Brightest</u> , which both explained the hubris that trapped us in that quagmire and created a phrase, in the title, that became common usage.

After that, Halberstam began alternating between very serious books, and books about sports. His book on basketball, <u>The Breaks of the Game</u>, is one of the best books on sports ever.

Through that book, Halberstam came to know Bob Ryan, the Globe sportswriter who had spoken at Masconomet. When I told Bob how much I admired Halberstam's work, Bob said "I'll get you his number."

---

[68] If you are going to plagiarize, you might want to be a little more subtle.

When I asked Halberstam to come to Phillips Exeter, he said, "Bob Ryan is such a nice man. I'll do it."

So Judy and I got to take Halberstam out to dinner after he got off the boat from his summer place in Nantucket, and drive him up to Exeter. My kids got to interview him in class, and over lunch. Halberstam addressed the whole Summer School at a weekly assembly.[69]

---

[69] I also had Bob do that, as well as Jack Driscoll, the editor of the Boston Globe. I was stunned that none of the Exeter Physical Education department bothered to go to hear either Halberstam or Ryan. Gym teachers.

Two things from Halberstam that have really stayed with me involved Bill Walton and Bill Bradley.

Halberstam had profiled Walton in the basketball book, and remained friends with him. As we drove to Exeter, he told us that Walton, then in the days following his playing career, had just called him. Walton didn't really know what to do with himself, and was contemplating becoming a spokesperson for a large car dealership.

Halberstam urged Walton not to sell his name that way, and urged him to consider something that would keep him in contact with the game, such as coaching or doing color or play-by-play broadcasting. Except for periods when his back's pain laid him extremely low[70], Walton has been broadcasting ever since.

On the ride up when we picked him up from the Nantucket ferry, I told Halberstam that I could relate to his sense of the last hope being extinguished when Bobby Kennedy died. I inquired whether there were any politicians or leaders who gave him hope at the time (1987).

He described wealthy friends going to Senator Bill Bradley of New Jersey, and telling him they had the money to support him, if he chose to run for president.

Bradley stared out a window silently for a long time, and then finally said, "Not yet. I'm not ready yet." Halberstam said that

---

[70] Walton recently revealed that the pain had made him contemplate suicide.

Bradley's humility and self-awareness made him think Bradley might be the next great hope.[71]

Halberstam's life ended far too young, a few years ago. A journalism graduate student at Berkeley was driving Halberstam, and ran a stop sign. Halberstam died instantly, when his side of the car was struck. The graduate student actually served time in prison. Still, I can't imagine the prison sentence could compare with carrying the knowledge that your impulsive judgment had silenced a voice like Halberstam's.

———————————————————————

My last summer, I was installed in a student room, on the top floor of a non-air conditioned dorm. It was brutally hot that summer. So I could get some sleep, I returned home to our house on nights when I wasn't on duty. That I had this retreat to go to thoroughly offended the regular faculty member in the vastly cooler first floor apartment. She insisted I needed to be there every night, all night.

The last night of summer school was always the one with the greatest potential for trouble, since students took buses out in the morning, and our disciplinary options were much more limited. So the dorm head made a big production on the last full day of telling the kids what a wonderful sendoff the buses

---

[71] Bradley would time his presidential aspirations poorly. We could have had him as president, instead of choosing between an Al Gore compromised by his association with Bill Clinton and a George W. Bush, compromised by Richard Cheney and the neocons.

would be in the morning, and how she would probably go to see them herself.

And then she left for New York that afternoon.

After my first summer at the Academy, the athletics department was kind enough to give me a locker in the faculty locker room year round. This was helpful, in that I had been sneaking in to use the athletic facilities since we moved to Exeter full time when I was at UNH. In the faculty locker room, I got to hear the politics of the place. The bickering and infighting at least equaled what was going on at Masconomet. But beyond the eight hours a day Masco required, most of these people were in the dorms full-time, and eating meals together.

This was less like immersion and more like being trapped on an island.

So, by the last summer I worked at Phillips Exeter, a place that had seemed so alluring to a young teacher had lost its' allure. There are certainly many advantages to private schools, not the least of which is that the students are paying to be there, and can be dismissed if their actions indicate they don't really want to be there.

The resources, and the tradition, of America's top private schools are matched by very few public high schools. At any private boarding school, the opportunity for greater immersion in, and impact upon, student's lives is enormous. For someone with the energy and the commitment, boarding schools may be a great place to start.

But I got older, my energy diminished, and my interests outside teaching expanded. I'm grateful that the experience at Phillips Exeter Summer School let me determine that Exeter would have presented its own issues, if I had landed there.

Things always work out for the best.

Chapter 8

Veritas, sans Gravitas

I came to Harvard to work with the teacher training program because of journalism, South Boston High School, and Jerry Winegar.

I was very impressed with what Winegar seemed to be accomplishing in a difficult situation at Southie[72]. That had made me explore the idea of becoming a principal. I interviewed a number of people to discuss the idea. By the last of the interviews, I knew that I could be a change agent as a principal, but that it would be at the cost of my personal life. By the time of the last interview, I had permanently ruled out administration as a career path.

When I met with Pat Graham, who was the Dean of the Graduate School of Education at Harvard[73], she asked me to meet with Kay Merseth. Kay was heading up the Mid-Career Math and Science program, training professionals from other fields to become teachers.

---

[72] I say "seemed to" because a friend would end up working there within a year, and there was apparently less to Winegar than met the eye. Jerry was a good self-promoter, but not good enough to keep him from being removed and placed in a dead-end job in the central office in Boston.

[73] Graham asked me to apply to the Doctoral program in administration. Given everything I had heard in the interviews, I just laughed.

I guess I was getting a tryout when I was asked to be on a panel responding to a national report on education. It wasn't the seminal <u>A Nation at Risk</u> report, but one that followed soon afterwards. I ran around interviewing teachers about some of the proposals in the report, since I was tasked with presenting the practitioners' response.

The response I heard from the people I interviewed was something like, "A lot of good another report is going to do me."

Accordingly, I started my speech with a joke along those lines, something about the cavalry coming but never actually arriving.

I could tell from the look of the panelist who had actually worked on the report that she was not amused.

I've never been fearful of public speaking, because of the role model my father represented. As a little kid in Springfield, I saw my father go on television. This was black and white television, in about 1960, so being on television was really special.

He told my sister and me that he was going to look right at the camera and smile just for us, and, sure enough, he did.

When I was in high school, he came home one night from a dinner where he was one of the earlier speakers. He had sat next to the main speaker, who was the radio broadcaster who had filed daily reports heard worldwide from London during the Battle of Britain[74].

When my father spoke, he gave a short speech extemporaneously, with no notes.

When he sat down, the main speaker leaned over to him and said "How can you do that? I'm terrified every time I have to speak in public."

This was a man whose voice was probably the most-listened to in the entire world at one point.

I'd also seen my dad give many graduation speeches, including at my own graduation. He always seemed comfortable speaking publically.

So I never felt a need to be fearful myself. In fact, any microphone has always drawn me, like a moth to a flame.

_____

Kay asked me if I would be a teaching practitioner in her program, specifically working with the chemistry teacher she had coming in the next year. I was a little surprised[75], but the allure of being associated with Harvard was a powerful draw.

The evening of the first class in the fall, I killed the afternoon hanging around Harvard Square. Sitting in an ice cream shop, I read about a psychological study into what was called the

_____

[74] I think this was Lowell Thomas.

[75] Does that qualify as humility? If so, that was a pretty rare sighting.

"imposter syndrome". The study had interviewed people at top level academic institutions like Harvard and Stanford, and found that many were driven to work inordinately hard by fear. Their fear was that it would be discovered that they didn't really belong there, and they would be removed once they were exposed.

That night, after leading her class, Kay said to me, "Did I do alright?" Here I was, just a high school teacher on his first day there.

I knew then I could do Harvard stuff just fine.

It may have been the confidence with which I said things in class that made the students seem to regard me as a font of wisdom. Or perhaps it was just the legitimacy of Harvard that Kay had bestowed upon me that made them react that way.

In any case, it was pretty heady stuff. I provided a picture from the Harvard class to the local newspapers covering Masco, and they wrote stories with Harvard in the headlines. The stories were entirely self-serving. I relished the thought of the reaction they must have produced in my Masco tormentors.

At one point after I began working at Harvard, my department head said to me, "You know, some people find you intimidating". I was never sure that he wasn't talking about himself in that statement. In any case, it struck me as ludicrous that I should be held accountable for the insecurities of others.

Kay asked me to be a teaching supervisor for the one student training as a chemistry teacher. This student was a teaching brother at Catholic Memorial High School in West Roxbury.

I took personal days from Masco, noting in the application that I would be off doing supervision for Harvard. The environment at Catholic Memorial left a strong impression on me.

First, I was struck by the indentured servitude of the teaching brothers. They lived right there, had social lives around the school, and were paid far below the levels of public school teachers. For an administrator, it would be a dream work force. For the teacher, I wasn't sure it was the best environment for personal growth. Over the year, he would reinforce that impression, as he confided that he wasn't sure he wanted to stay in the brotherhood. If he didn't, the certification Harvard was providing would give him mobility to move into public schools.

The second powerful impression was of the difference between public and Catholic schools.

Catholic Memorial was an all-boys school, with a long tradition of excellence in athletics. As I watched the adolescent boys pour into Tom's room on the first day I was there, I was struck by how the single sex formula seemed problematic. With no females around, the interaction of the boys coming in seemed like the type of locker room interactions a former teacher I admire refers to as "grab-ass".

But the transformation that followed was enlightening. When Tom started the class, he mentioned that they would be praying for a student's mother who had cancer. He mentioned other members in the community for whom they would be praying, and then they did the Lord's Prayer together.

And, with that act, the boys were transformed. They went from a barrel of monkeys to a focused learning community in about two minutes.

If there was ever an argument for the inclusion of prayer in schools, I saw it there.

Around the same time, I had gone to a number of funerals in my wife's Catholic family. During the mass, I saw the community building that occurred when parishioners would turn to one another and say "Peace be with you," and respond, "And also with you."

Because of that, I started a routine of having students, once they had come to know me for a month or so, stand up in class and turn to one another to say, "If you need help, I will help you," and responding "And I, you." I explained the Catholic origins of what we were doing, and that I wanted them to be a community of learners.

Some students got it immediately. Some got it down the road. Undoubtedly, some never got it.

I also came to see the unvarying routine of requiring students to do the Pledge of Allegiance daily as unproductive. So I tried to find ways to make that time period meaningful. During the week of Lincoln's birthday, I would read a paragraph a day from the Gettysburg Address, so the students could focus on the majesty of the words. The week of Martin Luther King, Jr.'s birthday, I would do the same thing with the "I Have a Dream" speech.

I'm fortunate to have had the opportunity Harvard gave me, to get out of my classroom, and see things in a different light.

In the first year at Harvard, there were really smart students. However, one in particular lacked the crucial attribute of "with-it-ness" that I first heard Kay articulate there. Although this student had designed the sewer system of Cairo as a civil engineer, it was clear that his spaciness was going to get him destroyed in most classroom situations. At the end of the year, he asked me to write him a letter of recommendation, and I begged off. I think I used the fact that I hadn't supervised him as a reason why I couldn't write an effective letter for him.

I don't think I had the courage to counsel him out of teaching, and I don't know that it was my place to do so. But his depressive personality, combined with his ethereal awareness, meant that the classroom was going to produce a lot of misery for him.

When I told Kay that I felt he shouldn't have been admitted to the program, she offered to have me interview applicants for the next year's class. I loved the opportunity, and all of the class members in the next class seemed to have the natural assets to succeed in the classroom.

I did my third year at Harvard running on fumes. What had been so prestigious at first became more of a chore. At Masco, we were moving forward in the battle over the Copernican Plan. I was grateful for the opportunity to be at Harvard, and sit in on Al Shanker's class, and spend a couple of hours being interviewed by MacArthur fellow Sarah Lawrence Lightfoot.

But what I was bringing to the class at Harvard was a much lower level of enthusiasm, and even alertness, than I had started with. This did not go unnoticed by Kay, and after the third year, she didn't ask me back.

Ironically, soon thereafter, Kay took a leave from the program. Her replacement in the course was the practitioner who had specialized in physics while I was there. He had a doctorate- which Kay had told me I should get if I ultimately wanted to replace her.

I'd had enough graduate work in education at Stanford, so I had no interest in a doctorate.

When Kay's replacement was setting up the course for his first year in that role, he left a message for me, saying he wanted me to return as the chemistry practitioner.

I never returned his call.

Chapter 9

Towards a Better Union

When I was getting my Master's degree at Stanford, I developed the idea that teachers' unions and tenure were both bad for education.

So, when I began my full-time job, I declined to join the teachers' union. The local was affiliated with the state teachers'' association and the national NEA. When I had asked Ralph, whose room I was in for part of the day, what protections the union could offer me as a non-tenured teacher, he said that there were none until I got tenure. I wasn't exactly sold anyway, but that closed the door for me.

It turned out that a very high percentage of the faculty were in the union. If wearing shirts with the Stanford logo on them didn't convey the impression of my sense of superiority, not joining the union certainly did.

The guys I carpooled with some that year were in the union. I liked them, although one of the regular riders was prone to make statements that were so poorly thought out that they left me speechless[76]. They didn't try too hard to sell the union, and, in fact, were critical of some of the dominant union leaders.

---

[76] In faculty meetings, Sid used the terms "erronous" and "fruital". I have spelled those words more-or-less phonetically, because it is hard to be certain of the correct spelling of words that don't exist.

Over time, my resistance wore down, and, in my second or third year, I joined the union.

As I read the mailbox bulletins from the local, I was amazed at how few voices were guiding the group. The same crew tended to rotate through positions of leadership, and usually ran for office unopposed.

I think you can see where this is going.

I decided to run for president of the local. I asked to see the salary schedules for the past few contracts. As I graphed how salaries had changed for each step and level of education, a clear pattern was evident. For quite a while, the union had been putting much more money into the top of the salary schedule.

When I asked Jon, a crew-cut major player in the math department and the union, for an explanation, he gave me one that seemed entirely self-serving. Since all teachers moved to the top of the salary schedule with time, it was of the most benefit to the largest number of members to put the dollars there.

While I saw his point, I felt that the future of the school would be most impacted by getting the best hires possible each year. As the community became aware of the high caliber of the evolving faculty, it would make negotiating salary and benefit increases for everyone easier.

Okay, I could be self-serving myself.

So I generated a "white paper" for distribution to the faculty, announcing my candidacy for president, at a time when the union hadn't roused a slate of candidates. The paper included data on salary increases, and why I felt they needed to be redistributed toward incoming hires.

I also expounded on how we needed to have professional goals as educators, goals that would improve the education of students, while simultaneously making our professional lives better. A good place to start would be in contractually limiting class sizes.

And, just for good measure, I described why we should be looking at alternatives that would allow the elimination of tenure. The guaranteed nature of tenured positions was surely distasteful to people who lacked such security in their own jobs. If we showed that we were willing to have the same level of job security as the common Joe voting in our school community, that also would make them more likely to support our goals.

In my uninformed idealism, I had neglected to learn that teacher tenure laws were part of the laws of the Commonwealth.

I probably had ten or fifteen people come up to me to say that they strongly supported my ideas.

And, out of a faculty of perhaps a hundred, those must have been the only ones who voted for me.

That should have been an adequate clue to me about the nature of the culture I was in. However, my reaction would be that the culture itself would need to change.

When I started there, Masco had no initiative to help beginning teachers. Any mentoring that was going on was the result of the efforts of individual teachers, and I was not on the receiving end of any such outreach.

But it was in the area of merit pay that the school had really gone wrong. And, of course, I would ultimately run headlong into that problem.

Negotiations between the union and the school committee had created two levels of merit pay: Associate Master and Master Teacher. Each provided additional stipends that came on top of the regular salary schedule.

And the merit pay status also gave additional protection in the contractual layoff language.

The program was voluntary, but if you didn't get merit pay status, you could be laid off before someone with less seniority, if they had attained merit status.

Since the program was voluntary, this created something of an ethical, if not legal, conflict of interest.

In my first years at Masconomet, there was a demographic bulge that was the proverbial pig passing through a python. Enrollment would decline over the years that followed.

After my first year, Mark, a chemistry teacher I sometimes carpooled with, took a two year leave of absence to teach in Europe. He actually got a sabbatical, with a year's salary spread over the two years, to be paid on top of his salary in Europe.

Because enrollment was still high, Masconomet hired a teacher to replace Mark in his absence. Harry was an extremely bright, energetic and intense teacher. His intensity caused him to speak too rapidly in class, and his intelligence made him lack much sympathy or understanding for struggling learners.

I worked with Harry to smooth out the rough edges. He was grateful for help and support. I even diffused a situation that could have been extremely detrimental to his career. Harry was an intellectual, with a born antagonism toward jocks. In a class where he was using a Tesla coil to electrify a cathode ray tube, Harry applied the coil to a very large jock, who hadn't volunteered to be shocked.

When the jock protested in pain, Harry impugned his manhood, and shocked him again. Fortunately, the jock didn't dismember Harry. He did come to me, since we had exchanged weightlifting tips, to say how angry he was to be treated that way. Given that his father was an assistant superintendent in

Peabody[77], the potential for a damaging complaint was huge. I talked Ron out of any complaint, and nothing came of it.

So, after three years, I received tenure, and was now eligible to apply for Associate Master status. When I took my application to Mr. Richards, the principal, he told me about the layoff protection it would give me. He said that it would be better to apply another year, because the district would prefer to retain the option to lay off either Harry or me.

Richards and I were still on reasonably good terms at that point, so I guess I should have seen him as doing me a favor.

Instead, I was outraged. I assured him that, if merit pay meant anything, I should be getting it, regardless of layoff language. I also thought that it would be ludicrous for the district to turn me down after Richards's warning, since it would point to a biased evaluation, but I kept that to myself.

So I submitted my application, and was given three evaluators. Richards was one, my department head Johnson was the second, and, for the third, they picked the next older department member, a female biology teacher.

Although she was young, Jeanna was strong-willed. Years later, she would describe herself to one of my students as being "a

---

[77] Who had worked under my father, when my father was staggering to the finish of his career.

bitch".[78] I'm not sure what her feelings toward me were; she once told me she saw me as like the Hawkeye Pierce character in the TV show "MASH".

However, she did do me the favor of telling me that Johnson and Richards had said she didn't have to worry about voting against me, since the two of them could reject my application. They told her this in the fall, before the evaluation process had even started.

In the spring, the vote was 2-1, against my being granted Associate Master status. The votes fell exactly as you would predict.

There was no appeals process allowed, but somehow I got it in front of the school committee. Surely, they would want to know how the administrators were operating.

In my first of what would be many appearances before the school committee over the coming years, I laid it all out for them.

Nothing changed. Conveniently, their hands were tied by the contract.

So, the next year, both Harry and I applied for associate master status. I got Johnson and Richards again, but this time my evaluator from the faculty was Lee. Mark, who held my

---

[78] For someone who saw herself as a feminist, this self-characterization seemed ironic, since she would have seen it as sexism, coming from a man.

teaching in high regard, was also available, but, amazingly, they picked Lee instead.

Although Lee busted my balls some in evaluating me, he ultimately voted to grant me Associate Master status.

Which didn't matter, because Johnson and Richards again voted no.

And Harry received associate master status.

The writing was now on the wall.

Or the chalkboard.

_____

It was during the merit pay process that I first learned of, and employed, the grievance process that was part of the contractual language. There were many steps to the process, and different levels at which a resolution might be reached. If the resolution wasn't satisfactory, the teacher could appeal to the next level up, ultimately ending in binding arbitration.

I won the first grievance I filed. Richards had violated the contract by keeping his own personnel file on me, which was not open to my inspection, and which he didn't reveal until he used material in it against me. The first level of grievance was to appeal to Richards himself. He didn't feel he had done anything wrong, so it moved up to the superintendent. Richards had been increasingly trying to expand his powers, and the superintendent may have been trying to reign him in by supporting me in the grievance.

Other faculty members were so impressed with my victory. That might be because, in the years before and after that, I was never aware of any other faculty member even filing a grievance, although that may have been because the grievance process was confidential.

Or it may have been because the grievance process went on for such a long time. Any teacher filing a grievance faced contractual timelines that ran for weeks, and potentially months, if the appeals process went to higher levels. All during that time, that cloud of stress would hang over a teacher, who still had a daily workload. And during that time, any interaction with the management would have heightened stress.

Over the years, I would file grievances against two department heads, two principals, and one superintendent.

That first victory was just a skirmish.

In learning about the history of American education while at Stanford, I learned about people like John Dewey, who had helped shape the education system. In the early 1970's, it seemed that the country was in need of a new visionary, for a system to evolve with rapidly changing times.

At the same time as I was in college and graduate school, that visionary was emerging.

His name was Albert Shanker.

Shanker had led a strike in New York City that made him a prominent local figure. As such, he became an inside joke in Woody Allen's "Sleeper." The film was about a man who awakes after a Rip Van Winkle-like sleep, to a future that follows a great war. When the character asks how The Great War began, he is told "A man named Al Shanker got hold of an atom bomb."

That was kind of a New Yorker's inside joke when the film came out. However, Shanker rose through the ranks of the American Federation of Teachers to its top. The AFT was more of an urban educators association, more likely to play the hardball of city politics. The NEA seemed to look down its nose at the AFT.

However, Shanker evolved as an educational reformer, and took the AFT along with him.

I read about Shanker in places other than the tedious publications I now received as an NEA member. He worked with progressive local affiliates, including Rochester, New York, to promote ideas such as mentoring and merit pay.

When I was working at Harvard, Al Shanker was hired to teach a course one day a week. In addition to what I read about Shanker in the print media, I had been reading Shanker's column in the Sunday New York Times.

The AFT paid for the column- it was labeled as "advertisement" each week. That Shanker recognized the value of spending AFT money each week on the column impressed me enormously.

What he wrote impressed me even more. The union organizer now had a breadth of vision in education that seemed unmatched.

When I heard that he was coming to Harvard, I asked Kay Merseth if I could sit in on Shanker's class. Kay forwarded my request to the Dean, who said I should ask Shanker himself.

So I called the AFT national headquarters in Washington.

Shanker answered the phone himself. No secretary, but Al himself. I told him how much that impressed me, and he said he did it regularly, since sometimes the secretaries might be busy.

He agreed to let me sit in on the class.

It proved to be the best class in education I ever had.

While he talked about many topics[79], one vision in particular fascinated me.

Shanker described a book on the standardization and professionalization of American medicine[80]. He described how the treatment for Lincoln on his deathbed had been delayed, while the doctors argued over competing schools of thought.

Then he described how doctors, and the formation of the American Medical Association, had elevated the medical profession in the public's eyes. While the recipe wasn't simple, this was one reason why doctors earned so much more than teachers.

He saw this as a map to transforming teaching. National certification standards for teachers should be developed, with many stakeholders providing input.

This was a man with true vision.

Some years later, when I worked to oversee Massachusetts' development of curriculum frameworks in math and science, the AFT released a report card. It graded all the states' efforts towards curriculum frameworks in math and science.

---

[79] There was one topic he wouldn't address. When he was talking about the strike in New York, I raised my hand and asked if he wanted to tell the class about his being mentioned in "Sleeper". The tone of his "No!" indicated he didn't think Woody Allen was terribly funny.
[80] The Social Transformation of American Medicine, Paul Starr

Massachusetts received the highest grade of any state, an A minus.

That meant a great deal to me.

Let me return to the premises that I got from graduate school-that both tenure and teacher unions are bad. My experiences certainly moderated those views.

The term "tenure" has become almost a boogeyman. If tenure is merely due process and just cause in dismissals, contracts can do that.

If tenure guarantees academic freedom, an argument perhaps more suited to post-secondary education, developing a national curriculum and assessment may reduce the need for such protections. A teacher working within the framework of a national curriculum, and assuring that students meet assessment standards, is probably going to have a fair amount of leeway in doing so.

If tenure is a method of preserving teachers in amber, so that they don't have to develop professionally, and stay current on national trends, that is a problem.

However, if systems are in place to update practitioners, stimulate new thinking, and allow for rejuvenation after years in the field, maybe tenure isn't needed.

If tenure was eliminated, so that less productive teachers would be weeded out, then the issue of how they would be replaced arises. There will be many applicants for most job openings in English, Social Studies, and Physical Education. But try filling an opening in math, science, or special education, particularly in a small rural or dangerous urban school.

Unions get the blame, more often than not, for protecting tenure. If unions became the professional organizations that Al Shanker[81] envisioned, tenure might be unnecessary. Organizations that certify, educate, and, when needed, sanction their members would elevate the teaching profession.

All that is needed is leadership. And commitment. And money. And top notch people entering and upgrading the field.

While the prospects for those things are bleak, they may not be more bleak than the long range prognosis for a failing educational system.

For me, tenure, and the teachers' union, saved my job on more than one occasion.

---

[81] There is a fairly good biography of Shanker, entitled Tough Liberal, by Richard Kahlenberg.

Chapter 10

Having Relations with the Public

Schools need to sell themselves. Private schools have to bring money in, whether by appealing to students, parents of potential students, or alumni. Private schools specializing in special education must sell themselves to districts that would foot the bill for students placed with them.

Public schools need to sell themselves also. Taxation as guaranteed revenue is less assured now than ever, in an era when the politics of "no" seem to rule. Furthermore, districts periodically have to use bond issues for major projects.

So public relations should always be on the agenda of every school, not just when budgets come up for a vote.

I never cease to be amazed that public schools don't understand that.

For a teacher, Parent's Night is a crucial opportunity for building support. Initially at Masco, Parent's Night came later in the fall, but eventually they realized it was important to get support early.

I always planned in detail what I would say in the ten or 15 minute slices of time we got in front of each class's parents. Some of what I was saying mirrored what I had said to students on their first day in class. You are trying to sell yourself, your curriculum, and the program, and do this all within time limitations you didn't have with your students.

I'd emphasize the importance of homework, which would be on the board behind me. I'd speak up for the quality of the text, because parents could reinforce the utility of that resource. I'd tell them that I was demanding, but list the skills the course would provide if students applied themselves e.g. reading, critical thinking, problem solving, and writing.

In science, I would emphasize the importance of lab safety. In saying that it would be unfortunate if their kids learned nothing, but totally unacceptable if they got hurt, I assured them neither of those things would happen.

Parents' Night attendance directly correlated with the level of the class. Honors classes would be standing room only. College prep would have some seats open. The lowest level classes would sometimes have no parents in attendance.

I always told kids in advance to urge their parents to attend. When a student would come up the next day and say that his or her parents had really liked me, I knew I had one more tool in my belt.

Schools need to have well-cultivated relationships with the media that covers them. In the tiny Vermont town where we currently reside, the school budget has failed twice in public votes. There is one paper regularly covering the town. That paper has struggled to find reporters to cover the little school.

It shouldn't have to look. The administration should be providing print-ready press releases all year long. There is a second, larger paper in the county which doesn't cover our town. The administration should be besieging them to cover the school, and making it easy for them with press releases.

At a school committee meeting about the unpassed budget recently, the members were bemoaning the misinformation in the town about the school budget. A simple postcard sent out by opponents of the budget had had devastating effect. Although the district had sent out a multipage flyer about the budget, it wasn't very well done.

The effort to get public support should have been year-round. The responsible parties for that, the administration, sat at the table with the school committee.

As a teacher, I didn't count on administration to do their job in public relations. It served my own purposes to do it myself. Every teacher should see that as part of their job.

Many teachers at Masco felt it was not their responsibility. If you are not going to be all in, you ought to get out.

My first year at Masco, I tried to call every home in the first month of school. This was not made any easier by the fact that there were only two phones made available for staff use. While

I made calls during free periods. I eventually had to start making long distance calls from my home, at my own expense. Most parents said they had never had a teacher contact them at home. Many figured I was calling for something bad.

I explained that I was just introducing myself, and hoped to have their support. If I ever did need to call with concerns, those initial calls increased the likelihood I would get parental support.

In future years, I replaced those phone calls with written communication to parents, which I would insist students had signed before returning them.

In my first quarter at Masco, I found that we had to send out failure warnings at the middle of the quarter, for any students who might get a D or F. This paperwork guaranteed grade inflation, since any teacher who had not bothered with the cover-your-ass exercise was less likely to give a D or F when it was earned.

My reaction to the exercise was to ask the principal where the commendation notices were, to be sent out at the same time. In a reaction that characterized his leadership and intellect, he said I should just cross out the words "Failure Warning" at the top of the form and write "Commendation" in by hand above that.

The man had a genius for public relations.

So I generated a commendation form of my own, sent them out, and agitated for a commendation form to be created that all teachers should be urged to use.

I encountered resistance from colleagues who saw commendation forms as one more bit of paperwork being forced upon them.

These were people unburdened by any excess of enlightened self-interest.

In future years, I started sending home mid-quarter reports on every student.

Some colleagues indicated that they didn't always have enough grades recorded to provide a mid-quarter assessment. I never had a response for that, but I suspect the look on my face conveyed a great deal.

Sometimes, in my early years at Masco, I couldn't find an ear to turn to in my frustration with a particular policy. Twice, I made a questionable choice in writing letters to the editor of the Tritown Transcript.

One was about the existence of a smoking area for students. It still staggers me that the school would make the concession to bad health to keep smoking limited to an area that could be monitored. Allowing students to do something that was harmful to them, during the time when they were our responsibility, was educational malpractice.

It wasn't in loco parentis. It was just loco.

A second policy that spurred a letter had to do with allowing students in good standing to leave school in their cars during lunch and free periods. The administration justified it by saying it was a reward for their responsible behavior.

I said it was an accident waiting to happen. The day would come when a student rushing back to school during the school day would be injured or killed.

When my dad became superintendent in St. Paul, Minnesota, he reversed a decades-old policy of never cancelling school, no matter how adverse the weather. He justified it by saying that it was worth it if the injury or death of one student had been prevented. Minneapolis followed his lead, and snow days have been celebrated ever since.

It is worth noting, however, that when he was driven out of that job five years later, some people saw that decision as having precipitated his downfall.

My letter provoked a letter in response, from a school committee member. He cited the importance of students learning, and benefitting from responsibility. I had initiated the public dialog, and his letter looked rather like I was being publicly chastised.

It was no more than two years, and maybe only one, before the accident occurred. A student who I had taught, and really liked, was in a crash rushing back to school. He wasn't killed, but suffered neurological damage that would be with him for the rest of his life.

In loco parentis.

———————————————————

Through journalism, I developed contacts at the local papers. This gave me specific individuals to whom I could send print-ready press releases. I could also let them know about stories I hoped they would cover, and usually got a story and photos in papers when I contacted them. They actually seemed quite eager for the stories, and it seemed no one else at the school was providing them with story ideas.

I know some of my colleagues saw what I was doing as self-promotion. They were absolutely right. When Dr. Brown worked hard to try and fire me, he was trying to fire someone who had a clear public identity. There is a power in secrecy, and my having a public persona took away some of his power.

But my self-promotion also benefitted the school. People complain there is only news when something bad happens. With schools, the media is more than happy to publicize good things happening. It is just common sense to make it easy for them. Then, when bad things do happen, the negative impact upon the school has been blunted.

I let the media know about guest speakers in class, field trips, students I had who were going to Phillips Exeter Summer School, awards my kids had gotten, my work at Harvard, and students' letters written to Reagan on scientific issues of the day. I can't actually remember a story I pitched or sent as a press release being turned down.

When the vote of confidence was taken against the superintendent, I urged my colleagues to be more pro-active in public relations, since the struggle was going to be very public[82]. Al Shanker's columns in the New York Times provided a model.

I went to the Tri-Town Transcript and urged them to run a column from educators at Masconomet. Since I had helped make Masco a hot topic at the time, they bought it.

---

[82] I had made sure of that myself by notifying the papers about the vote of no confidence. Operating in secrecy was a power I wasn't going to allow him.

As vice president of the teachers' association, I urged everyone in the Masconomet community to contribute columns, including the superintendent.

I wrote a column to get it started. The superintendent wrote one that was not exactly impressive. An English teacher and writer who was the association president wrote one. I wrote another, and pleaded with my colleagues for more, so we could make it a weekly feature. Another teacher, who had journalism experience, wrote one. I wrote yet another.

And then there were no more from my colleagues. I may have submitted one more that the paper chose not to use, but the paper decided to stop running the column.

We had wasted an opportunity.

Which is <u>exactly</u> what public relations represents.

Chapter 11

What the Sabbatical Wrought- On the Plus Side

When the school committee crammed my sabbatical down the reluctant superintendent's throat, he felt compelled to act like he was supporting the initiative.

Watching him "explain" the need for the sabbatical to the school committee, I heard him say that, since I would be working with the CHEMStudy program in Berkeley, I would have to be out of school, since they were so far away.

I had never suggested that I needed to be in Berkeley to do the work. I planned to do the work in our newly built log cabin in northern Vermont. I guess I could have corrected him, but it was just not my nature to publicly correct one of my superiors.

During that year off, we drove around the country in our van, accompanied by our four Boxers. We did stop in Berkeley, to see the nonagenarian director of CHEMStudy, Dave Ridgway. While we were there, he took us up to the Lawrence Hall of Science. There he brought us to the office of Glenn Seaborg, the Nobel Laureate who had overseen the development of the CHEMStudy program.

I think Dave was delighted to show Seaborg that the program was being resurrected. New segments of each film were being shot that year, and I was producing materials that had never existed before to go along with the new editions.

The walls of Seaborg's office were covered with photos of him with government officials. Seaborg had grown up in a Midwestern town, inordinately tall and inordinately smart. He was probably a prototypical nerd long before the term arrived on the scene.

He worked on the Manhattan Project as a young man, and later was involved in the discovery of numerous elements in the Transuranium series, at the bottom of the periodic table.[83]

The walls of Seaborg's office were covered with photos of him with celebrities and government officials. Five or more

---

[83] Among the elements were the place-named Californium and Berkeleium. It has been suggested that he should also have discovered Universitium and ofium.

presidents were there, along with British Prime Minister Margaret Thatcher. Thatcher may have been more thrilled at meeting Seaborg than the other way around. As a young woman, Thatcher had worked as a chemist. She was part of a team that invented soft-serve ice cream.[84]

Seaborg served as a science advisor to many Presidents, from Truman through the first George Bush. While we looked at the pictures, I commented that it must have been hard explaining science to some of the Presidents who weren't versed in the subject.

He smiled when I mentioned Reagan specifically. Then I said that the current office-holder, Bush the Elder, had to be better at understanding science, given his Yale education.

He merely rolled his eyes, as if to indicate that Bush didn't grasp science either. I didn't pursue it, since he seemed to be trying to be diplomatic.

When my materials were finished and published the next year, Dave Ridgway sent the film notes on the Transuranium series to Seaborg.

I had put in information that I got from library research.

Glenn Seaborg had actually been there.

---

[84] Not the Manhattan Project, but with a lot less downside.

So, Glenn Seaborg, the only man to have a chemical element named after him while he was still alive,[85] wrote corrections on my film notes.

In red ink.

So I have materials I produced, with the handwriting of a now deceased Nobel winner on them.

Saying I'm stupid.

---

[85] Seaborgium, element number 109. You could look it up. Or, if you are Rainman, you already knew.

It didn't take a Nobel Prizewinner to make that observation.

And yet, I couldn't be prouder.

Transuranium Elements Film Notes

$$_{96}Cm^{246} + _6C^{13} \longrightarrow _{102}102^{254} + 5_0n^1$$

Nobelium was suggested for element 102 by Swedish scientists at the Nobel institute in Stockholm then later was adopted by the American ~~by the American~~

~~Element 102 was named Nobelium by its Swedish discoverers at the Nobel Institute in Stockholm, Sweden. The name was accepted after Russian claims to its discovery were rejected.~~

$$_{98}Cf^{252} + _5B^{11} \longrightarrow _{103}Lr^{257} + 6_0n^1$$

The accepted symbol for Lawrencium became Lr. It was named after Ernest Lawrence who invented the cyclotron at Berkeley.

$$_{98}Cf^{252} + _6C^{13} \longrightarrow _{104}104^{261} + 4_0n^1$$

Element 104 will probably be named after Lord Ernest Rutherford, who did important early work in radioactivity. This element was also discovered at Berkeley. Final acceptance of an element's name is decided by the International Union of Pure and Applied Chemistry (IUPAC).

Possible new element synthesis

$$_{99}Es + _{20}Ca^{48} \longrightarrow \ ?$$

Synthesis of element 109

$$_{83}^{209}Bi + _{26}^{58}Fe \longrightarrow _{109}^{266}109 + 1_0n^1$$

The half life of this element, produced by West German researchers in 1982, is milliseconds.

Why make these expensive, synthetic elements? Practical applications: Plutonium served as the power source on the Voyager probe to Neptune. It might also serve as an energy source for cardiac pacemakers.

246-4156
© 1991 Ward's Natural Science

Chapter 12

The Great War

Because high schools typically have science requirements that students fulfill by their last year or two, there is a filtering and winnowing that occurs in science courses. In a typical sequence of physical science, biology, chemistry and physics, you see the whole student population in the first course, and a vastly smaller and more select population by the time they might get to physics.[86]

Similarly, having courses with multiple tracks allows students to move up or down to a level appropriate to their potential achievement. Most of that movement was actually downward, so students who weren't succeeding would go to lower levels.

As the squeeze increased after my first few years in the science department, I was assigned to teach physical science. I was not pleased at this latest scheduling snafu. Although Lee was the last person I should have expected as a sympathetic ear, I lamented being assigned something other than chemistry to him.

---

[86] Dr. Post, as department head, reversed the sequence for advanced students, with Chemistry Honors preceding either Biology Honors or Biology AP. Although I think biology logically precedes chemistry in developmental terms, this gave the former college professor an older and more select group to teach. This was not only self-serving, but vastly undermined his validity as a supervisor.

His response was that the contract I'd signed said "teacher", not "chemistry teacher". It actually seemed like a pretty valid point. It seemed rather self-serving, however, when I later found out that he had come to Masco as a physical science teacher. Apparently, he wasn't inclined to return to that level.

Teaching a couple of mid-level freshman physical science courses wasn't too bad, however. The book was lousy, and, again no one could explain why it had been chosen[87]. The course was guided by Ralph, a teacher approaching retirement whose enthusiasm for teaching had clearly waned. Therefore, we were doing largely the same activities and labs.

I wasn't really happy to be doing the physics half of the course, but it was pretty low level stuff. There was stuff about machines and levers that I had a hard time understanding and applying, but I explained that to the kids, and they were always good about helping me see how to apply the ideas.

When I returned from my sabbatical, I was assigned two physical science classes. However, this time they were the lowest level. That was drastically different from the midlevel course I'd taught before. Because kids needed to meet a science requirement to graduate, every student was in physical science. Whereas I had previously taught classes that might have a few special education plans for students, now virtually

---

[87] In a much larger district, where textbook adoption represents a vastly bigger expenditure, I would have suspected someone got a kickback. However, in a tiny district like Masco, kickbacks would have represented an absurd financial model for textbook manufacturers.

every student in both of those classes was in special education. One student was very challenged physically, and prone to drooling all over himself. This provoked open disgust from some of the other behaviorally challenged students.

Jenny was particularly cruel to that young man. I spoke to her, and then disciplined her, but the cruelty didn't stop. I wasn't even sure how cognizant her target was of the cruelty, but I wasn't about to assume he was missing all of it. There were other disciplinary problems in the same class section. None of these kids seemed to have experience being held to on-time arrival, or doing homework, or paying attention.

As the Great War raged on that year, I was getting overrun. I started looking for help. State special education regulations seemed to indicate that, given the number of special education students, I should have been getting help in the classroom. Instead, I was always going to special education meetings on one student or another. The meetings themselves filled my time, but not my students' needs, as they provided nothing to make a difficult situation better.

When I sent a memo indicating the district seemed to be out of compliance in not providing classroom support, Dr. Brown responded with some weak justification for the district's inaction. I might have pursued that further, but there were always new memos to respond to, new evaluations to rebut, and not enough time.

Fortunately, I discovered that, since I was certified in neither Physics nor Physical Science, having me teach more than one class of Physical Science was clearly in violation of state regulations.

The solution to that was that the two classes I had were combined into one larger class.

Dawn, a sweet and conscientious student who was in the better of the two sections, came to me very upset. "I was so happy to get away from those kids, and now we're going to be back with them again!"

I told her that I couldn't bear up under my class schedule and the other demands on my time, and that combining the two classes was the only solution the district offered. She was much less happy for the rest of the year.

And I just hung on. Jenny[88] would threaten to shoot me, or that her father would shoot me. When I took that to Steve, who was principal, his response was that I didn't need to worry, because principals got shot much more often than teachers.

But her threats finally got Jenny removed from my class. At least she couldn't torment classmates- or me- anymore.

I made it through that school year. And, because I found out about the state regulations, I was never assigned more than one Physical Science class a year afterwards.

---

[88] I chose this particular alias because of an Aerosmith song, "Jenny's got a Gun."

The source of my final departure would come from a Physical Science course, but that story was much more complicated.

And, by that time, my departure had been a long time coming.

It wasn't a man obtaining an atom bomb that started The Great War[89] at Masconomet. It was a man, or two, actually, who wanted a sabbatical.

During the years of layoffs at Masconomet, my own included, sabbaticals became something of an afterthought. When my first superintendent returned to his home state of Vermont, he was replaced by Dr. Brown, who had headed a large district in Florida.

Economic conditions improved, I returned to the science department, and I started thinking about a sabbatical.

After all, I had taken a year off, at my own expense, and returned rejuvenated and productive. Certainly any teacher could benefit from a similar hiatus, particularly one where they left feeling the support of the district.

---

[89] In calling my struggle The Great War, I am in no way comparing it to what people truly experience on the battlefield. I have always been grateful for the high draft lottery number that meant I wouldn't find out how I would hold up in combat. I will say, however, that both my father and I experienced our own form of PTSD as a result of our careers in education.

Dr. Brown didn't agree. In conversations with him, he had various reasons why he wouldn't support sabbaticals. Perhaps the lamest was that he had once been burned by a teacher who took the sabbatical money and never returned. The truth may have been that he was thinking that the cost of a sabbatical would take funding from his own agenda.

So, initially, he said I couldn't present a sabbatical proposal to the school committee, since he didn't support it.

It turned out that Dr. Brown's choking autocracy had been why he was fired in Florida, but no one in the union had bothered to be involved in the selection process that chose Dr. Brown. Therefore, the nature of his firing, which would prove predictive in his troubled tenure at Masconomet, didn't turn up until I made some calls to Florida, at the height of the Great War.

What Dr. Brown didn't take into consideration as he blocked my access to the school committee was that my father had finished his career in Massachusetts.

When I told my dad that Dr. Brown wouldn't let me present my proposal to the committee, Dad[90] said what Dr. Brown was doing was illegal. Dr. Brown couldn't block my access to a public meeting.

Presented with this fact, Dr. Brown conceded, and told me I should come to a specific meeting.

---

[90] I'm writing these words on Father's Day. Thanks Dad, for this, and all the other ways you helped me.

So I wrote up a great spiel about the values of sabbaticals, what I would do, and how all teachers needed such rejuvenation.

Then, when I got to the meeting, I just sat there. The chair of the committee was just about to close the meeting- because Dr. Brown hadn't put me on the agenda, which he clearly controlled. I waved my hands furiously. I saw Dr. Brown act as if he had just noticed my presence, and whisper to the chair, a community member the local union despised.

Dr. Brown said I wanted to make a presentation for a sabbatical proposal. On cue, the chair said this was not the place for such a presentation. It should have been done during the meetings on the budget (when Dr. Brown was blocking me), and therefore they would not hear my proposal at that time.

I could briefly address the committee about sabbaticals in general, but nothing about my own proposal.

I looked at the carefully developed presentation in my hand, and then ad-libbed about sabbaticals in general. And, when the meeting was over, I walked over to the reporters for the three different newspapers covering the meeting and gave them a copy of my prepared remarks.

Large portions of the prepared remarks were printed verbatim in the local papers.

The next day, colleagues came up and praised what I had done.

The next year, I turned the sabbatical proposal in to Dr. Brown even earlier, and he was forced to include it in the budget hearings, although without his support.

That way, the committee got another chance to turn it down.

I wasn't done, though.

_____

Dr. Brown was busy trying to draw support for an educational reform that I'm sure he thought would be the crowning achievement of his career.

I'd seen this before. At the peak of his career, in St. Paul, my father had started developing ideas for community educational centers, which he called City Centers for Learning. In a way, they would be predecessors to what are now called magnet schools, with each center specializing in a specific type or area of learning. They would also be resources for the whole community, with facilities that all could share. And they would provide a way for St. Paul to integrate its schools.

Oh, yeah, and they would have monorails. That last bit may be why the Disney Corporation had him come to consult on Disneyworld, and their planned community of Celebration[91].

My father drew heat for spending public money on his fantasies, at a time when the cities were erupting and federal funding was shifting from The Great Society to the great

_____

[91] It would be the next town over from Stepford.

mistake that was Vietnam. The final product was a book that laid out all that City Centers for Learning could be. It was published a month after my father resigned from St. Paul, to go back to Massachusetts, so he could retire from there. That book gathered dust on the shelf in the house in Exeter for decades, until I finally pitched it.

So that was yet another way that my father had been preparing me for conflict with Dr. Brown.

Dr. Brown's level of grandiosity didn't compare with my father's. Fundamentally, he wanted to restructure the school day, with longer blocks of time for each class, so learning could be more concentrated.[92] This would allow for more efficient learning, as well as less time lost passing between classes. As a small handful of Masconomet teachers joined him in idealistic speculation, they also came up with ideas like community forums on important topics.

And there may have been a monorail in there, somewhere.

The vast majority of Masconomet teachers had no interest in Dr. Brown's "Copernican Plan"[93]. Particularly in the math

---

[92] You can read about his brainchild, in an article by the man himself. He humbly titled it "The Copernican Plan Evaluated: The Evolution of a Revolution". It is in *Phi Delta Kappan*, Vol. 76, No. 2.

[93] Copernicus said the sun was the center of the planetary system, not the earth, just as the student would truly be the center in Dr. Brown's plan. I think Dr. Brown would have named the plan after himself, but he figured Copernicus had better name recognition.

department, where innovation wasn't gaining any foothold, the idea of longer classes was ridiculed.

Since the union powers also were largely seated in the math department, obstruction of Dr. Brown's plan became modus operandi for the union.

I, myself, had no problem with it. Dr. Brown asked me to teach in it, on three different occasions. I was wary of getting involved in a crisis of someone else's making, so I always turned him down.

Dr. Brown had initially said he wouldn't implement the program unless the vast majority of teachers were on board. That ship sailed with a very short passenger manifest, so then his proposal became a "pilot program".

Having gone back on his word to go with "the vast majority", he now was working to get students who would volunteer to be in the program. He promoted the program in the community by saying only the best teachers would be in it.

Another brilliant sales strategy for drawing in his unsupportive faculty.

A recruiting pitch for students was that they would be able to get their homework done in school.[94]

All the while, the funding for the program was being questioned, both by faculty critics and those school committee

---

[94] Rendering the term "homework" oxymoronic.

members who seemed to feel some responsibility for fiscal oversight. Dr. Brown chased after grants and foundation money, but never found his sugar daddy. The question kept being asked about how he was going to fund this program.

As the bigger scheme was downsized to the pilot program, Dr. Brown also tried to give it new life, by changing the name to the Renaissance Program. I think he hoped the House of Medici would step up with some funding.

As I watched all of this with a certain amusement[95], another teacher put in for a sabbatical. Derek was a kind and gentle Social Studies teacher whose Christian faith probably guided his commitment to teaching the lowest level classes.

When Dr. Brown turned him down, he had a new reason. Sabbaticals were only for the best teachers, Dr. Brown said, and Derek couldn't be one of the best teachers, since he taught the lowest level students.[96]

Derek was hurt and offended. Enough so that he stood up at a union meeting and described his experience with Dr. Brown.

I saw an opening.

I was really tired of the obstructionism to Dr. Brown's plan. It didn't seem like that big a deal to me, and it was paralyzing the school. Like the situation Obama faces today, everything coming

---

[95] Okay, it was outright glee.

[96] A rare bit of candor in which the values of management were revealed unadorned.

from Dr. Brown was now subject to savage criticism, rather than rational reflection.

I thought it was time for the union to put up or shut up.

So I stood up and said that, if the union could not work with Dr. Brown, they needed to make that clear. I suggested we take a vote of confidence.

I didn't think there was much chance they would go for it. I was hoping that would then lead them to the "shut up" part of the equation, and maybe the school would move forward.

Yet again, my analysis of human character was completely wrong.

A cry rose up, in response to my words, akin to the moment in horror movies when the villagers get their torches and pitchforks.

Jon, the crew-cut eminence of the math department and the union, said the wording for the vote, and ultimately, the whole effort, should be led by Dave, the key voice in support of the Renaissance Program, and me.

I'd created a monster of my own.

But we threw ourselves into it, including Derek, as well as Rick, a young teacher whose idealism had been totally misplaced when he joined the math department.

Dave, Derek, Rick, and I also decided to form a slate of officers to head the union. Much to our surprise, we met with no resistance from the old guard. I suggested Dave be president, as his support of the Renaissance Program would make him a less threatening figure to lead us. I took vice-president, Derek was secretary, and Rick was the treasurer.

The union voted an overwhelming vote of "no confidence" in Dr. Brown. We sent the document to him and the school committee, and awaited a response.

When response seemed slow and limited, I went, off the record, to the paper most read in the community. I sat down and told them what was happening, and asked that my name be kept out of it.

When that hit the papers, Dr. Brown suddenly got a lot more responsive.

As vice-president, I had volunteered to attend school committee meetings, and speak up on issues affecting the faculty. What I saw in the meetings was distrust and dysfunction. Some of the male members seemed to fully support Dr. Brown's autocracy. Some of the female members openly distrusted him, and said as much, on the record.

In fact, they feared what he could do. Early in his time at Masco, Dr. Brown had overseen the dismissal of Jay, a long time guidance counselor.

Jay had made himself a target over a period of years. His student clientele included most or all of the students who were in special education[97]. Perhaps because of that, his office was next to the Life Skills Lab, and far from the actual guidance department. Operating in his own little orbit there, he took to burning incense in his office. That was probably part of his own cultural drift, as he told me that he wondered what it would be like to come to work stoned.

He tangled repeatedly with Richards when Richards was principal. Jay was a big, athletic guy, and undoubtedly made the much smaller principal aware of it. When Jay was president of the union, he had circulated a survey on morale, entirely of his own making. That personal touch was evident, in questions like the one that asked whether stress at Masco had impacted the respondent's sex life.

The old guard was undoubtedly not very supportive of Jay in such actions, and that would ultimately mean he had been effectively separated from the herd.

Then it would just be a matter of time until the predators finished him off.

As he became more unstable, Jay told me that he knew people who could be hired to kill Richards. Like everyone else, I tried to keep more distance from Jay.

Another teacher who Jay tried to enlist for support told me that Jay would show him memos from the administration that were clearly trying to set Jay up to commit dismissible offenses. He

---

[97] By the superintendent's reasoning, this would have made him a bad guidance counselor.

would point this out to Jay, and Jay would charge into the traps anyway.

When it got before the school committee, it was a spectacle. Although it was in executive session, one of the women committee members who was openly opposed to Dr. Brown described it for me. She said Jay had begged for his job, crying, saying "I don't want to lose my job."

Needless to say, he did.

The reason the committeewoman told me about this was that she "had seen what Dr. Brown can do." She warned me that tangling with Dr. Brown would be detrimental to me, and that she didn't want me to end up like Jay.

It was eye-opening that she feared Dr. Brown, but her distrust wasn't the most publically visible sign of his fractured relationship with the school committee.

Because Dr. Brown would oversee the production of minutes from the meetings by his secretary, I watched as members insisted that all meetings be taped, because they felt that Dr. Brown was rather too liberal in his editing of the meetings.

The deadline for sabbatical proposals approached, and no one, including Derek, was putting in for one. Conveniently, I was able to pull one together.

And, this time, the committee bought it, unanimously. The people who distrusted Dr. Brown saw me as an ally. The people endorsing fascism probably saw it as a small price to pay to get me out of there.

When Dr. Brown had to suggest some minor cuts in the budget, one of the things he proposed cutting was my sabbatical. This time, they roundly rejected his proposal, with one of the members snapping, "You shouldn't have even brought this to us!"

So now I had a sabbatical.

That wasn't hard, was it?

The summer when I started my sabbatical, I got a letter from Dr. Brown saying that a special needs student I had advocated for, Toby, and his needs, were not my business, and I should not be inquiring about them. Jim, a member of the Special Education department who ran the "alternative program", was at my house that day, and we both looked at the letter in puzzlement.

I had been advocating for a few hundred dollars, in books on tape, for Toby. To my astonishment, and without my knowledge or involvement, Toby ultimately became an expensive outside placement at the Landmark School (and would be admitted to the University of Michigan and make the Dean's list after that).[98]

Upon returning from the sabbatical, I got a couple of classes filled with special ed plans. One student in particular, who would threaten my life on more than one occasion, seemed in need of an outside placement. Don, her special needs teacher, said he had brought that up, but that they got mad at him because it cost money.

The reason why that money was important became evident at a budget meeting the year I returned from sabbatical.

When Brown was asked to explain a revolving account in Special Needs, Richards, who was both assistant superintendent and district treasurer[99], sprang forth saying he could explain it.

---

[98] I had cost the district some serious bucks before that, though. Jason was wheelchair-bound, but loved working at the school radio station. The station had been built on the second floor, and the radio station advisor used to bring Jason up the steps. Someone saw that this represented a huge liability, if someone got hurt. The school's solution was to tell Jason he could no longer work at the radio station. I don't know how I heard of this, since I never had Jason in class, and barely spoke to him. In any case, I told Judy about it. She pointed out that the school could lose any federal funding it got for denying him access.

I told Jason, and told him to never mention that he heard it from me. Over the summer, the radio station was moved to the first floor, and Jason continued working there. I don't think I was ever connected to that one, but who knows?

[99] His appointment as treasurer was justified as a cost savings. It also eliminated a set of eyes who might be auditing how the district spent money and complied with state regulations.

Richards was hardly a verbal genius[100], but he proceeded to talk at a speed just short of that of a tobacco auctioneer.

He said that it was a revolving account, taking in tuitions from special needs students from outside the district and paying out for any outside placements. He said that because our special needs department was so good, we always had a surplus, which could be revolved to anyplace else in the budget.

Since the school committee was constantly asking Brown how he could pay for his "Copernican Plan[101]", I can guess where that money was going.

When Richards finished his explanation, I asked the Parents Advisory Council president next to me what she thought he had just said. Her response was "That's a slush fund."

No journalist picked up on the explanation- and it took me awhile to make the connection myself.

I later called the Department of Education legal office. They said that Commonwealth laws on regional school districts

---

[100] As principal, Richards once came on the p.a. after a fire drill, and thanked the students for the speed with which they had "excavated the building." I could dig it.

[101] About this time, Dr. Brown went before a class at Harvard to tout his plan. A superintendent from Alaska with whom I had grown friendly in Al Shanker's class asked Dr. Brown if he wasn't from the district where Dana Dunnan worked. As my friend praised me and raised questions about the resistance Dr. Brown was meeting in the district, he said Dr. Brown looked as if he were passing an exceptionally large and rough stone.

required that unspent special needs funds be returned to the towns.

So it wasn't merely an ethical breach, but malfeasance that may have been criminal.

That got lost under the onslaught that I faced from Dr. Brown and his minions. As Dr. Brown targeted me, I countered with grievances at every opportunity. At one point, he had guidance start interviewing every one of my students, on a fishing expedition for complaints to use against me. Given his bias, he had them start with my top students, who quickly objected. When they contacted their parents the interviews stopped.

Special needs faculty were fishing around among my lowest level students, and their nets pulled up a few more fish that Dr. Brown felt were adequate to merit suspending me.

And the war was on.

———————————————————————

It was a war that would last over two school years. Endless meetings, hostile and demanding memos to respond to, and I still had to teach. Dave, a junior high Social Studies teacher and the grievance chair of the union, was a buddy with whom I played basketball in the morning. More than that, he was a stalwart ally.

I saw the strain in the behaviors of my department chair, Dr. Post, and the principal, Steve. I had once considered them allies, people I trusted. Operating under Dr. Brown's direction, they did things that earned them grievances. Dealing with Dr. Brown's vendetta against me was taking a huge portion of their time.

I can remember seeing Dr. Post talking in the hallway before school with a school committee member who was also a lawyer[102]. I heard enough of the conversation to know that he was being advised on how to deal with me. The look on Dr. Post's face when I came around a corner confirmed that.

Memos flew from Dr. Brown, Dr. Post and the principal. Sometimes I'd have to sign for registered letters sent to my home, an intimidation tactic that only served to enrich the Postal Service. Often they were clearly intended to set up the kind of traps that had gotten Jay dismissed.

My refusal to fall for the traps, and continued contractual assaults on them, were not going unnoticed by my colleagues. Dr. Brown's power moves, such as how he reorganized the management team, and, more intimidatingly, fired Jay, had made him the scary figure he hoped to be to faculty.

I was undermining that. One day, he stood at a podium, waiting for the faculty to finish filing in before he addressed them. Having received the latest broadside via memo that day, I walked up to him and snarled "If you think I can be intimidated, you are very wrong. I've seen a better superintendent in his underwear, and he never intimidated me."

---

[102] Around this time, he took on a high profile case defending someone who was absolutely reprehensible. Probably not pro bono, either.

As I said this, Dr. Brown's eyes darted around the room, hoping that my insolence wasn't being heard. Then he realized he was standing in front of a microphone, and he struggled to find a switch, in case it was on and this was being broadcast.

It wasn't, but I saw the fear in his eyes, the fear that everyone would see what the wizard behind the curtain really was.

I laughed and walked away.

At the outdoor Memorial Day assembly that year, there was the crackling of fireworks on the school roof. While the entire high school watched, the tar on the roof began burning.

As we waited for the fire trucks to arrive, one of my students said to me, "Mr. Dunnan, you must have done that!"

It might seem evidence of the paranoia the war had induced that I told the student to not even joke like that. She looked a little surprised at the insistence in my response; I was a guy who supposedly had a sense of humor.

When I entered the high school office once we could return to the building, one of the secretaries said the editor of the local paper was on the phone, asking to speak with me.

I was astounded when the editor asked me if I had anything to do with the roof fire. I asked where she had gotten such an idea.

She wasn't willing to reveal sources, exactly.

But she did tell me she had just been speaking with the superintendent.

Finally, in the second year, Dave thought there was an opening for a truce. The suspension was removed from my record, the money withheld returned to me, and it was over. The school district had spent $35,000 dollars in legal fees alone.[103]

But I outlasted Dr. Brown. Within a year, he was pushed into retirement. The Renaissance Program was gone.[104] In his last attempt to get the program in play, he offered to take a salary of a dollar for a year. As eyeballs on the committee rolled, he said that he was willing to do so in exchange for the program being imposed school-wide. The head of the art department, who was sitting next to me at that meeting, agreed that Dr. Brown's proposed salary met the definition of merit pay.

I should say that I am glad to have had the experience with Dr. Brown. At that point in my life, I would still have defined myself as, first, a teacher. From then on, my first goal was to be the best husband I could be. Adversity Judy and I have faced, not just from Masconomet, has tested us, and always made our relationship stronger. I know that she is far and away the best

---

[103] Brown had once threatened to have "his" lawyer go after me. It turned out that he was referring to the district's lawyer, who he saw as there only for his bidding. And, apparently, the bidding got up to $32,000.

[104] Ironically, statewide ed reform in Massachusetts would push schools into longer teaching blocks soon thereafter.

thing that could have happened to me, and I give thanks for and to her every day.

I also am blessed in that my professional and personal self-image came from many sources other than Masconomet. Professional success at Stanford, Harvard, Berkeley, MIT, Phillips Exeter, and the state and federal departments of education merely made the contrived criticism of Masconomet diminish my critics in my eyes.

That Judy always believed in me sustained me, too.

When I stood up to Dr. Brown, I felt Masco could be a better place, one superior to the under-performing culture comparative state testing was showing it to be.

I felt it was a place worth standing up for.

And, if I didn't stand up, how could I expect anyone else to do so?

Without the financial burden of kids, confident I could find another job if need be, it took less courage for me to stand up than it would have for many of the colleagues who I at times criticized for their silence and complacency.

But dealing with Dr. Brown made me suspect that the problem was much larger than one man. And, if so, the problem might be inherent in the culture of the school and the surrounding community.

In which case, maybe it wasn't a battle worth fighting. I think I might have affected the climate at Masco for a while. However, culture runs much deeper than climate. There was never the critical mass of people needed to change the culture.

When community member and former school committee member Bob Forney was doing undercover work on my behalf in the Great War, the chair of the school committee, Paul Lindquist, told him that Masco only had two problems: the troublemakers Dana Dunnan and Bill Spencer.

Bill could battle from deeply held Christian principles.

I was probably going more on ego.

I could see questioning my motives. But that anyone would impugn Bill Spencer- well, clearly something was wrong here.

Chapter 13

Outside Variables

With the expansion of laws impacting students over the past decades, there has been an expansion of special education services. My own experience with special education at Masco found them of questionable use, but I knew how much better they could be.

In my first years at Masco, special education was focused on the life skills lab. This was a room equipped with beanbag chairs that special education used as a drop-in center, while regular students were in study hall. It hardly appeared to be a whirlwind of academic activity, as students seemed to just be hanging out.

Over the first years of my career, special education came to require a formulated educational plan for each identified students, and meetings where those plans would be discussed with, and, hopefully accepted by, parents. Teachers would describe how the students were progressing in the class, which would be incorporated into the report.

Unfortunately, the plans were poorly written, laden with terms endemic to special education, and absent any useful suggestions to implement in the classroom. A teacher who moved from Social Studies to Special Education greatly polished the plans on which he worked, thanks to his writing skills.

However, that still left the plans absent clear classroom strategies.

This teacher moved into special education through a program designed to address shortages in the field. Regular classroom teachers could take courses to gain the certification, so he and one of the gym teachers made the switch.

What never changed in my experience was getting special education staff into my classroom to help. Even when I had classes that were filled with ed plans, I was still the only educator holding the fort. Masco's special educators were more inclined to urge reducing the expectations for their students, and enable their unproductive behaviors.

The main reason I was always so critical of the Masco special educators was that I knew how much more they could be doing. My wife was always in classes with students, and wrote voluminous reports on them that included viable suggestions for the classroom teachers. I saw the materials she produced at home to help students in their classes, while I never saw anything of that nature in 26 years at Masco.

I think Masco's primary goal in special education was to avoid the cost of outside placements. The alternative program retained kids who might have been tuitioned out to schools for behavioral issues. Another program took students with the most severe physical and mental challenges and kept them at Masco, up until adulthood in some cases. Masco's programs drew students from other districts, and brought in tuition with them.

I was only aware of one student ever having been tuitioned out of the high school. I never thought he needed such a major adjustment, but the small modifications I suggested certainly raised the superintendent's ire.

Special education is an example of the kind of mandates that have come to be imposed on our schools. Underfunded, or unfunded, they broaden the scope of what schools are asked to do, without broadening the financial foundations of the schools adequately.

Another department that could potentially support classroom teachers is guidance. At Masco, guidance seemed to have college admissions as its top goal. Since that is a visible measure of success, that may make more sense than trumpeting the personal guidance and support that students were being provided.

Unfortunately, the Masco guidance department seemed to be averse to students receiving rejection letters, so, in my experience, they tended to discourage students from reaching for better schools where they might be more likely to be rejected. Instead of "Aim high, reach for the stars!", it was "Make sure you don't miss!"

It would have been helpful if students with personal issues could be directed to guidance. Unfortunately, many students had little faith in their guidance counselors, and were unlikely to turn to them. When I suggested that students see their counselors for issues that I felt were beyond my competence, I was likely to get eyes rolled at me.

Coaches can be enormously influential in students' lives. While teachers are getting students because of requirements, athletes are usually in a sport because they want to be there, and love the sport.

I took courses at UNH on coaching football, basketball, and track. I helped coach freshman football at Woodside. The coaches at Woodside were centered in the Physical Education department, and I used to walk down the corridor to join them for lunch.

The Woodside coaches were intelligent, thoughtful, and respectful of their students. The head football coach told me that he didn't ever practice for more than two hours, because kids would be too tired to learn effectively at that point. The basketball coach integrated minority students being bused in from East Palo Alto into his program, showing sensitivity to how different their lives were from the privilege of most Woodside students.

Woodside produced many division 1 college athletes, Olympians in numerous sports, and athletes who had professional careers.

What I found at Masco was very different. The military rigidity of the football coach was assuring mediocrity. The basketball coach was a racist, who rubbed the head of his first star player from the ABC program for good luck. The wrestling coach was given to screaming and swearing at his wrestlers, and once made a losing wrestler walk home from an away meet- in the winter.

The soccer and track coach was the only voice of reason among the varsity coaches. When his star sprinter wanted to skip his senior season and graduate early to travel around Europe with his sister, the athletic director was aghast. The coach encouraged it, saying would be a great experience.

Seeing who I would be working with, I never applied for any coaching positions at Masco.

Toward the end of my time at Masco, the chair of the school committee, whose son was on the basketball team, told me that the varsity coaching job was mine, if I had just applied. That was after years of playing basketball with the kids in the morning, and after school. The racist was no longer basketball coach at that point- in fact, he was now athletic director. I can only imagine what being basketball coach under him would have been like.

I played basketball with the kids out of love of the game. I had never played organized basketball, but grew to love it through pickup games with friends in high school.

When we played in the morning, the games were co-ed. A friend and colleague, who was in his 50's most of the years we played, and I would play together with the girls. ABC kids were usually among the boys. We also got boys playing who were among my smartest students. These weren't kids who were likely to try out for a sport, but they came because I was playing, and they felt comfortable. Our morning games over the years included two kids who went to the International Science Fair.

There were also kids who came back after graduation, knowing that we would be playing in the morning.

The best play I ever saw while I was on a court anywhere occurred one morning. A recent graduate, who had started at quarterback in football and guard in basketball, showed up for the first time. My colleague, who was a great passer, was leading a two-on-one break against the alum. Jenna was on the wing. She hadn't gotten much opportunity to play at the junior varsity level, and came in to play with us because she loved the game. Jenna curled around behind the defender, and Dave looked him directly in the eye- and bounced the ball between the defender's legs. Jenna, who had excellent hands, caught the ball as it came up off the bounce, and laid it in.

That guy never came back to play with us again. Gender equality can be hard for some males to accept.

Chapter 14

The Invisible Man, et alia

When I came to Masco, I was hired by the superintendent. He did the interview because the principal was on vacation, and the department head for my first year was still in graduate school.

If the department head had been there, I think he would have hired me. He was intelligent enough that we had a natural rapport. I actually considered him a friend for a number of years.

The principal might have hired me, if only because the other candidate was a woman. However, his fundamental insecurity might have made him detect that I might be a threat down the road. Aspirations for power like his require heightened survival skills.

One reason I suspect the superintendent hired me was that he had a son moving through the system who was already showing signs of trouble. We discussed my experience as the son of a superintendent, and he asked what he should do about his son.

I told him to get his son out of the school. It was difficult enough growing up anyhow; feeling like all eyes were on you only made things worse.

The superintendent did ultimately put his son in private school, but he returned to Masco, where I taught him. I got along well with the son, but I remember all-too-well when his girlfriend came to school with a black eye. There were also stories about the superintendent being attacked by his son, to which the bruises on the girlfriend's face lent credence.

The superintendent's hiring me was an abnormally high level of involvement in the school's functioning, based on the visual evidence I gathered over his tenure. While he would make an appearance on the first day for teachers, it would be brief. After that, he would seemingly evaporate, and I might glance him in the school once over the rest of the year.

This was amazing to me, given that the district consisted of a junior high and high school, which were adjoined. The superintendent's office was in a separate building, perhaps 20 yards away. In all of my dad's jobs before St. Paul, he spent at least a day in each of his schools. In St. Paul, where he was ensconced in City Hall, he still got out to the vast majority of schools in his increasingly tumultuous tenure there.

So I found it hard to have any respect for the superintendent. Within a couple of years of my arrival, I had begun calling him The Invisible Man. The name was immediately popular in my carpool, and had some currency in the rest of the school.

Never one to waste time, I demonstrated disrespect for the superintendent in my first month at Masco. In an unusual display of involvement, he invited all of the new teachers to meet with him in his office after school one day[105].

As we sat around the table, the superintendent asked if we had any questions for him. One of the other newbies prostrated himself in an outstanding act of brown-nosing.

"What would you expect to see if you came into one of our classrooms?"

The superintendent responded with, "I would expect a teacher to know the IQ's of every student in the class."

Now, the failings of IQ scores were well covered at Stanford. Furthermore, he was asking something worthy of Rainman, who didn't exist yet.

After my self-control had restrained me for perhaps a nanosecond, I asked him, "Oh, does IQ tell us that much about a student?" I'm sure I wore the mock-sincere look on my face that highlights my sarcasm costume.

The superintendent conceded that perhaps it didn't, and the conversation moved on to long-forgotten ground.

Over the superintendent's tenure, there were reports of his drinking. The guys in the car pool told of being in a bar when the superintendent, drinking by himself, toppled over backwards off his barstool. When it was announced that he

[105] It was not necessary for us to pack a lunch for the trip there.

would be leaving to return to Vermont, his valedictory at the high school graduation was much anticipated.

By the time of his departure, the consensus was that Richards was calling most of the shots, while in the high school principal's office. The school committee must have seen that as a problem, since the superintendent's successor, Dr. Brown, was clearly brought in with a mandate to rein Richards in.

On the day of the superintendent's final Masco graduation, he appeared to be pretty lit up. His remarks from the podium seemed to bear that out.

The superintendent chose to elucidate the accomplishments of his tenure. Showing his priorities, he cited the building of a brand new administration building, this one at the other end of the campus, perhaps 30 yards from the end of the building.

Then his oratory lifted off on a flight of hyperbole. He was leaving behind a school that was superior to any in the Commonwealth.

Nay, not merely the Commonwealth, but the entire country.

In fact, going all in, the whole world.

Clearly, this was not based on direct personal observation. Given how little time he had spent in the building, it was hard to picture his visits to the other schools of the Commonwealth, country and world.

But perhaps that's where he had been all along.

Visiting other schools.

When the new superintendent came, he wanted to establish right away that Richards was being reined in. He chose the first day with teachers to do that. Richards had been hovering around Dr. Brown obsequiously, all morning. He sat right up in front, barely restraining himself from kneeling when Dr. Brown got up to address his new faculty.

After beginning his speech, Dr. Brown looked down at Richards and said, "Richards, get me a glass of water."

Curtains fluttered as the audible intake of breath among the faculty dropped the room pressure significantly.

Richards was fully up to the task, as he returned with a glass of ice water on a tray, accompanied by a pitcher.

It was clear there was a new sheriff in town.

When Dr. Brown got to Masco, the structure of the administration was odd, but the potential for it to get odder still existed.

After a year in charge of the science department, Jones had been moved into a newly created position, assistant principal for curriculum. In this role, he was placed in a tiny office just off the high school assistant principal, who doled out discipline. That assistant principal had what I considered the worst job, in trying to deal with all discipline himself. A little more person power in that office might have made sense, but it would be many years in coming.

So Jones sat in his little office, visible to all, for years, until Dr. Brown arrived. What he was doing was unclear, but he clearly seemed to hold little or no influence. I felt badly for him, since he was clearly smarter, and seemingly more principled, than anyone else in the administration. I also felt badly for myself, since Steve had seemed to appreciate my teaching, and wasn't rendered insecure by my presence.

When Dr. Brown came in, Richards' position seemed really tenuous. My carpool acquaintance Sid reported seeing Richards sitting in his office in the early morning, dejected[106]. When Sid asked what was wrong, Richards replied that he thought he might be fired.

Richards looked stressed all the time, as the day when Dr. Brown was going to announce his restructuring approached. From the look on Richards's face, he didn't know what was coming, even as Dr. Brown strode to the podium[107].

Dr. Brown announced that Jones would be the new high school principal. Faculty applause probably reflected a release from Richards's heavy hand as much as amazement at Jones' elevation from purgatory.

---

[106] Sid was hardly an astute observer of the human condition. He was the most intellectually challenged faculty member not wearing a whistle.

[107] But I'm betting he had a pitcher of ice water ready, just in case.

Dr. Brown then announced that Richards would become his assistant superintendent for business. Given Richards's background as a typing and accounting teacher, this probably made more sense than his tenure as an insecure educational leader.

However, it was still only a two school district.

It wasn't too long before I convinced my journalism students to do a study of administrative costs at similar sized districts throughout the Commonwealth. As you would expect, it showed the absurdity of Masco's administration.

The story didn't win any awards.

But I'm sure it was richly appreciated in certain offices at Masco.

Two sweeping changes handed down from the administration show how the Masconomet culture was dysfunctional.

Detention was the primary disciplinary tool within a classroom teacher's toolkit. The problem was, when kids didn't come to detention, usually nothing would happen to them. To me, it seemed obvious that if you suspended kids for skipping detention, the detention tool would retain its efficacy.

Instead, the braintrust[108] came up with a demerit system. Students could be assigned demerits for numerous offenses, by the assistant principal's office.

For teachers, if a student skipped detention, you had to turn in his name, and the date of the offense, and the demerits would be automatically assigned.

This meant you had to make sure that the student was in school the day of the detention, before you turned in the demerit slip.

It added another layer of paperwork for the classroom teacher. And, just as old homes often had newspaper stuffed in walls as insulation, it added another layer of insulation between students and the consequences of their actions.

For many teachers, the additional layer of paperwork made it less likely that they would follow through on their discipline.

As for me, I can be as OCD as necessary.

Before I went home every day, I would look over my detention slips, and write up the demerit slips to be dropped at the office on the way out. With the secretaries in the assistant principal's office, I referred to myself as "The Demerit King". I'm sure second place wasn't even close.

The ultimate result of accumulated demerits could be a loss of privileges, or suspension. The braintrust added another layer of insulation from these consequences. Kids would be allowed to

---

[108] I use this term for the administration somewhat sarcastically.

go to teachers who had issued the demerits and ask if there was a way to make them up. If a kid had missed a detention, you could offer that they could have those demerits removed by serving a greater amount of time. I made my plea bargains so onerous that they rarely got accepted.

The attendance policy that was instituted had similarly developed principles. If a student skipped class, you would turn in paperwork, after checking the attendance list. A student could have, seemingly, unlimited legitimate absences. However, if a student got to six absences, if even one was unexcused or illegitimate, the student would be dropped from the class.

This added yet more paperwork and recordkeeping, which needed to be done at the end of the day. In my rankbook, I had to record every absence, and then I would go back and circle the unexcused absences when the absence list was circulated later in the day. As soon as I got to the magic number six, I would turn the accumulated data in, and there was a pretty high chance the kid would be removed from the class.

The level of recordkeeping this entailed seemed more than many teachers could or would do. I know I had many more kids removed from my class than any other teacher.

OCD has its own rewards.

—————————————————————

Although I believe these consequence-deferred policies came when Steve Jones was principal, he was a vast improvement over Richards. Steve had actually taught a difficult academic subject, biology. And, while he was principal, he actually returned to the classroom for a week, just to keep his hand in.

I may have partially inspired that return. Early in Dr. Brown's tenure, I issued a proposal, called management team substitutes. I wrote up the idea in a form that paralleled the writing style that Dr. Brown's memos to the faculty had taken. Dr. Brown's style reflected his Harvard education, and was unlike the rudimentary writing skills of most the administrative memos seen previously.

Although I had intentionally parodied Dr. Brown's writing style in my proposal, I didn't think it was so obvious that it would be much noticed. In the memo, I proposed that the superintendent and all non-teaching administrators should return to the classroom regularly as substitute teachers. I argued that it would help them stay in touch with the kids, as well as the realities of the classroom.

I also knew from my experience as a substitute teacher when I was at UNH that you could tell a lot about a teacher when you substituted for them. I didn't say that in my proposal, but I thought that, if the proposal were actually implemented, it would expose some pockets of teaching incompetence.

I placed the proposal in all faculty mailboxes just before Thanksgiving break. My colleagues loved it. The parody had been vastly more obvious than I realized, and was much appreciated. Furthermore, the sentiment that administrators had too much remove from the realities of the classroom teacher was widely shared. If I had run for union president at exactly that moment, I probably would have been elected.

I never got any formal response from the administration. Bruce, the junior high principal who was the personification of good-old-boyism, came up to me as I was monitoring hall behavior outside my classroom.

The administrators were far too busy to do substituting, he assured me. I think he also implied that I wasn't fully aware of the tremendous importance of their work.

I kinda thought I was, which was why I'd written the proposal in the first place.

The power brokering skills that brought Dr. Brown in to rein in Richards eventually made Dr. Brown himself a problem for the school committee. When Dr. Brown announced his retirement[109], the chair of the school committee was a man named Dave Forman.

Forman was the first person I'd ever heard who described himself as a "libertarian." I have come to know libertarians whose philosophy was intellectually sound. I suspect Forman

---

[109] In retirement, Dr. Brown would write a letter to the local paper supporting the Masco budget, signing it as "superintendent emeritus". I don't think Nixon in exile approached that level of self-delusion.

was the type of libertarian whose philosophy was largely serving his own purposes.

At the start of the second year of The Great War with Dr. Brown, Forman had addressed the faculty on opening day. He had criticized "troublemakers" at some length, all the while staring at me. I was fairly amazed, first that anyone would publically do that, and second, that he would think I was prone to intimidation after the War had raged on that long.

So, it sounded like grandiose ego when Forman announced that the school committee would search world-wide for the best possible replacement for Dr. Brown.

Shortly thereafter, the announcement was made that the new, world-class, superintendent had been found in…………

The assistant superintendent's office!

With Richards's appointment came enough irony to rebuild the American steel industry.

The deal appeared to have been cut that Richards would serve two years to enhance his retirement, and then retire.

It seemed that way to me, anyway, since, in his last two years, Richards was never anything but solicitous to me.

Having been away when Dr. Brown was hired, and seen what he had wrought, I was not going to let the next superintendent get hired without thoroughly investigating.

I was friendly with a school committee member who had attended UNH when Judy and I did. I hadn't known her then, but we had watched her cheering as her future husband played basketball for UNH. When I had discovered the UNH connection in conversation with her son, we had arranged to have supper together and go to a UNH game with her family. When we set up that engagement, I hadn't even known she was on the school committee, and I told her that I almost cancelled when I found out.

She would be my conduit to provide information to the school committee about prospective superintendents. When I got the list of finalists, I started making calls.

The leading finalist, in my eyes, was a principal in Connecticut. Because he had worked previously as a principal in Boston, I was able to call Jerry Winegar about him, and got a glowing report.

I also called the head of the teacher's union at the school in Connecticut. She hadn't known he was looking, but had nothing but great things to say about him.

That same day, I got a call from Richards, then playing long term lame duck in the superintendent's office. The Connecticut candidate had called him, apoplectic because he hadn't let anyone in his district know that he was looking, and now I had revealed it.

Richards told me I had caused a problem, and I explained that it just hadn't occurred to me. I think I even called the guy and apologized, telling him that I thought he was the leading candidate.

When I told my department head, Dr. Post, about my screw-up, I commented that I wasn't sure if Richards would feel compelled to take some sort of disciplinary action.

Dr. Post, who had really been worn down by his being an unwilling participant in The Great War, commented "I don't think Richards is planning on being around long enough for that to play out with you."

No action was taken. I reported to my friend on the school committee about how good the top candidate was, and she supported him.

There was a second candidate who I thought would be acceptable. Dr. Cavanaugh worked in Exeter as an assistant superintendent, and got good reviews from a union leader I knew in town. I think he even mentioned that she had been the point person for the district on sexual harassment issues.

My friend on the committee supported the principal from Connecticut for one or two rounds of voting. However, eventually she yielded to others on the school committee, including Dave Forman.

Dr. Cavanaugh would be our new superintendent, and the last one under whom I would work.

———————————————

I was pleased at the idea of female leadership. Richards's shortcomings as a leader seemed like they stemmed, in some part, from his being a male, and a short one who was overcompensating[110]. Perhaps the shortcomings of the other braintrust components were testosterone-related, also.

I personally welcomed Dr. Cavanaugh to the district, and thought she did a great job in her first year. The school committee's evaluation of her glowed. I even called the local papers to suggest a story on Dr. Cavanaugh, and that Masco's leadership troubles were behind it.

Dr. Cavanaugh was brought in to remove Steve as principal, among other things. Steve could appear lazy, phony and pompous[111], and he had built up far more critics than defenders.

I was probably naïve about Steve Jones from the very beginning. When he was in my first year, the edict came down from on high that all Masco teachers needed to be evaluated, and then rated as above average, average, or below average.

---

[110] Once Richards and I became adversarial, I always used to stand close to him when we talked, so it would be obvious that I was looking down on him. If I haven't been fully clear about it before, I fully understand how I brought a lot of my troubles upon myself. Part of the point of the book is so that others might choose to avoid making my mistakes. Or not.

[111] And maybe he was. I didn't find his persona off-putting, but when he fell in line with Dr. Brown in The Great War, my support of him was done forever.

Steve, being equally brand new, needed to come up with justification for such labels as he would be attaching to the members of his new department.

Steve asked me to do a self-evaluation. Earnest and eager, I produced a brutally honest self-evaluation, in which I was particularly open about my feelings of inadequacy in the subject of chemistry.

Steve asked if I would share the self-evaluation with him. Which worked out well for him, since he used it to justify declaring me to be below average among the three chemistry teachers. The criticism of my subject knowledge would linger for a long time, to be used as material in many future evaluations.

I did get some satisfaction, however, in watching the blowback from the assigning of the three labels. Mark was probably pretty typical of many veteran teachers, in that he took great offense at the "average" label, after his many years of teaching chemistry.

The administration then did some tortured damage control, as they told everyone how, because Masconomet was such an outstanding school, being labeled as average at Masconomet meant you were really an excellent teacher, relative to the rest of the universe.

The phrase "Masconomet average" was bandied around a lot in my first year. Then the practice of applying such labels to each teacher disappeared, without the intent of its original use ever being clear.

After a couple of decades at Masconomet, Steve was clearly falling short of the "Masconomet average" in his role as principal.

Dr. Cavanaugh leveraged him out impressively. Kids had written racist graffiti in the school. Steve had it cleaned up. Dr. Cavanaugh said he had destroyed evidence in a hate crime, and could be prosecuted. Faced with that, Steve suddenly decided to retire, at a comparatively young age. After he left, I would see him occasionally, glad-handing at Masco events, but he never got another job that I was aware of.

After my detective work[112] in seeking a new superintendent, I was eager to be involved in the principal search. Again, the union was willing to let me play that role, perhaps because no one else wanted to expend that kind of energy.

I was already getting some blowback from within the union for Dr. Cavanaugh. Union leaders would express their frustrations about her to me, blaming me for her getting the job. I didn't have any idea why at the time, but math teacher and union activist Alan Hand told me that he thought Dr. Cavanaugh was "an awful, awful human being." I figured negotiations had been

---

[112] Inspecteur Clouseau, at your service!

really ugly, but I would come to learn that his grievance against her may have been much more personal.

Ever the crusader for a cause, I thought it would be good if Masco continued the gender transformation of its management by getting a female high school principal.

I sat on the interviews with the finalists. One fellow wore a cowboy hat to the interview. Given that Dr. Brown had been famous for his turquoise neckpiece on his bolo ties, he was probably a goner before he opened his mouth.

But he and the other finalist didn't stand up as well as Andrea, a former principal from Nantucket who was at the Harvard Principal's Center. Nantucket is a small island, with a really small high school. I spoke to a school committee person, and to her daughter, who was at the high school.

Everything I heard from them sounded good, and I didn't get much positive on the other candidates.

Andrea became the last principal I would work under.

The set pieces for the end game were now all in place.

Chapter 15

MIT

As I developed a friendship with Ron Latanision at MIT, we talked about his hopes to contribute to public education.

A commitment to public education has been an all-too-rare commodity in research universities like MIT, Harvard, and Stanford. For professors on the tenure track, being a good teacher has been historically less important than research and publishing.

Ron was an excellent teacher, as well as highly accomplished in his field. When I met him, he headed the Materials Processing Center, and he committed resources at the Center to outreach to public education. Other professors in the Center weren't as committed to public education, so Ron ended up leaving the Center.

However, he continued to make MIT aware of his commitment to K-12 education. He probably gained some leverage for his commitment when he was offered the job as Dean of the School of Engineering at Ohio State, and turned it down.

In our talks, he asked what MIT could do that could most benefit science and math teachers. I explained that the mere access to MIT that I had received from him would be invaluable to teachers.

Based on my experience, teachers often didn't feel like valued commodities in their home districts. I had been able to come to MIT, access their universe of resources, and be treated with respect. If there was a way to do that for others, it would boost their status, and inspire them to greater things in their own classrooms.

With the help of a great secretary, Connie Beal, and a master of all resources, Jon Bartels, Ron began a summer program for teachers. I was asked to participate in the initial planning and development of the program. It came at a time when I was in the run-up to The Great War, and I declined, feeling I just didn't have the needed energy.

Ron, Connie, Jon, and others got the program off the ground, and the first class decided to create an ongoing connection between teachers in the program. Initially called NEST, for New England Science Teachers, that connection has brought hundreds of teachers to MIT, and thereby enriched the experiences of tens of thousands of their students.

I became more involved in the summer program, and NEST, as the conflict at Masco abated. I attended the summer program, and was active for years in NEST.[113]

Ron was supportive of my career in other ways also. At the height of my battle with Dr. Brown, Ron let me know that he

---

[113] Go to http://web.mit.edu/scienceprogram/nest/ for an overview of where this great program stands now. The newsletter is a door to many resources, including the summer programs for teachers that continue to expand at MIT.

would do whatever he could to provide support under the auspices of MIT. He continued to provide that kind of personal support right through my last days at Masco, and for years after that.

When I got my sabbatical, Ron had offered to find me an office at MIT, and a position as visiting scholar. I declined, because I planned to spend the year either at the cabin we had built in northern Vermont or traveling around the country. The toll Masco was taking made me prefer a retreat to the woods over advancing into the traffic of Boston and Cambridge.

I would use the visiting scholar status when I left Masco for two years near the end of my time there. Once again, that association with MIT recharged my batteries and restored my professional self-image.

MIT was an intellectual Disneyland for those two years, and for many years after that. I sat in on classes that interested me, and loved interacting with the students.

One class was on modern Russian history. There were two instructors, one of whom had been a journalist in the former Soviet Union in its last days.

He described being at a press conference with Boris Yeltsin, where his question, according to joking colleagues, brought down the Soviet Union.

In Russian, he had asked Yeltsin "Boris Nikolayevich, given that comrade Gorbachev is away at the G-8 summit, isn't it possible that you could take the reins of power, dissolve the Soviet Union, and leave him out of power upon his return?"

Yeltsin responded, "Good idea!"

In another class, I listened to a professor who was highly visible in the media for his ongoing criticism of missile defense systems. He was a very public critic of local defense contractor Raytheon, and, as such, was regularly appearing on the front page of the Globe.

I sat in on a seminar with a woman who had made it her goal to interview all the women leaders of nations around the world. I'd always felt that having role models was important for underrepresented groups, including women and minorities. She provided powerful anecdotal support for that belief.

Ireland had been headed by a female president for many years. She told of a mother who said her little boy had asked her a telling question.

"Mommy," he said. "Could I be president, or is that only for girls?"

The social significance of Obama's election cannot be overstated. It is too bad he had to defeat a woman to get elected, but their day is coming, perhaps in 2016.

———————————————————

While I was at MIT on a two year leave of absence, I faced a decision about returning to Masco. In the fall of the second year, it became apparent that the funding for a curriculum project to keep me at MIT wasn't going to develop.

I had to let Masco know by December if I would be returning. We had bought a house in Greenland, between Portsmouth and Exeter, soon after my mother's death in 1998. We thought that the huge house in Exeter would sell quickly; a potential buyer had appeared in our driveway within an hour of my putting a sign up on the front lawn. Unfortunately, we still owned the house in Exeter, and the cost of having both houses weighed heavily.

As the date for a decision about returning to Masco approached, my back began to cripple me. At times, I would go up the stairs to our bedroom on my hands and knees.

It occurred to me that the back problem might provide me with a way out of returning to Masco. However, I wasn't willing to endure the crippling pain for however long it might last.

I went to see our family practitioner. He was a great believer in the mind body connection, and, in fact, felt that almost all back pain was based in psychological issues like stress.

He asked what might be bothering me, and I described my dread of returning to Masco. He suggested that I take a drug called Paxil.

I was reluctant, having never taken any psychoactive medicine before then. But I trusted him, and it seemed that it might alleviate the back pain.

Within a week, my back was better. I found that the Paxil made the world a brighter place. Things rarely seemed to upset me, and I was happier.

I didn't even feel compelled to look for another place to teach than Masco. It was only a half hour from the house in Greenland, and I was so far advanced on the salary schedule that it was unlikely anyplace else within comfortable commuting distance could approach what I could earn there.

So I let Masco know I would be coming back in the fall.

After all, how bad could it be?

Chapter 16

Kids and Colleagues

The people you work around are a huge factor in your happiness in the workplace. In my time at Woodside, and Phillips Exeter, and MIT, there were bright stimulating people.

At Masco, it was harder finding such interactions. In my first year, there were older teachers, Bill and Ted, who headed the Foreign Language and Art departments, respectively, who were great to talk with. However, with most colleagues, discussions of books or world events were hard to sustain. Conversation about the Red Sox, however, was readily available.

Faculty lounges and lunchrooms are where information is exchanged and alliances are formed. That is harder in half hour long lunch periods, when it takes five minutes to get to and from the lunchroom, and, well, you do have to eat your lunch.

At Masco, the faculty lounge was eliminated long before I left. Strategically, that would be a great move if you were an administrator who gained power by keeping faculty uninformed and isolated. Or it could just as well be that you didn't care much about faculty morale.

Richards had a great moment at the end of a school year in which his leadership as principal had been criticized. After saying that he had a number of things he wanted to get off his chest, he ran through a list of complaints, usually about specific teachers[114]. He concluded by saying, "And, if you have a morale problem, it's your problem, because it's your morale."

That would look nice on a sampler.

Dr. Brown's vote of no confidence came at a time when my hopes for teacher professionalism were at an all-time high. I was sitting in on Shanker's class, and being inspired. My Masco colleagues, instead of just being whiney drones, had actually stood up for something. Dave, Derek, Rick and I were now the officers of the association.

I read in an AFT magazine about teachers at a Virginia high school who would meet socially outside of school to discuss articles and books that were professionally relevant.

So, I sent out an invitation to all faculty members to come to our house in Exeter for a discussion, mentioning specific books as topics.

The Saturday night arrived, and only Rick showed up.

How 'bout them Red Sox?

As I've said, Harry, who was hired when Mark left for two years after my first year, was very bright, and very intense. I think he had a really hard childhood, with a difficult father. Harry

---

[114] I don't remember if I made the list. I'd certainly like to think so.

attributed a bad back to the fact that his dad had made his kids dig a foundation for their house by hand, to save money.

That background also made Harry perhaps the cheapest individual I've ever known. His clothes were the barest minimum to look acceptable, his car was ancient, and he was always looking to save money. When he was in the carpool, we hated the days he would drive. Ever thrifty, he would not put on the windshield wipers or the headlights until the complaints had risen to the level of rebellion.

It seems reasonable to hypothesize that financial insecurity was a huge driver for him.

When he came to Masco, our department head was Mr. Johnson, a lazy good old boy whom the superintendent had recruited from Vermont. The fact that Johnson didn't know science made his supervision of Harry and me a little shaky. Soon, Harry and I openly shared our contempt of Johnson with one another.

I didn't take any crap from Johnson without a response, and Harry built himself up to the point where he decided he wouldn't either.

Then Johnson retaliated with a harsh evaluation of Harry. I was passing through the room where he was teaching when I was free first period. Harry waved me into the back room, closing the door on the students in his class. Then he burst into uncontrollable weeping, showing me the evaluation. He was sure they were going to fire him, what could he do, would I take his class?

I said sure, and told him to go home, that I would cover for him.

Harry left. I took his class, and called the office to get a substitute for him, saying he had left overcome by the flu.

I never told anyone about the incident.

And Harry never gave anyone any crap from that day on.

———————————————————————

After Harry left, Masco hired a young woman who had gone to Wellesley and then gotten her teacher certification at UMass. Paula was a bright, idealistic breath of fresh air, whose personality reflected her upbringing in Ohio.

She was the colleague I'd always wanted. She always wanted to talk about teaching chemistry, and education in general. Sitting in a classroom, discussing how to teach atomic theory, or stoichiometry, or how to do a particular demonstration, was exhilarating for me.

When she began teaching at Masco, I was doing teacher training at Harvard. Paula asked if I would arrange for her to sit in on the class, because she wanted to hear what they were discussing.

Paula stayed at Masco for about three years, I think. I watched her become more confident as a classroom teacher, and as a person.

Then she left, for a completely new challenge, to teach in an American school in Amsterdam. From there, she moved to a great private school back in Ohio.

When I talked to her after she left Masco, it was clear that her knowledge base in teaching had expanded far beyond mine.

Change and stimulation can be stressful. But they also can lead to adaptive growth, beneficial to the organism and its evolution.

The stress at Masco was certainly not beneficial to me.

I'm glad Paula found greener pastures.

There is an old saying, "Those who can, do. Those who can't, teach."[115] While it might be a commentary on people in a field, like the military, where disabilities prevent work out in the field or on the battleground, generally, the phrase is pejorative of the teaching profession.

Piling on, Woody Allen added, "Those who can't teach, teach gym."

I remember the sadistic gym teacher and swim coach at Highland Park, back in St. Paul, who pulled more than one kid out of the pool by their hair. This was the same pool in which all of the boys were forced to swim naked in gym class. It was an enclosed indoor pool, but we were chagrined to learn at future

---

[115] This is a slight variation on the original quote, from George Bernard Shaw. Ironically, Shaw wrote it in Man and Superman.

class reunions that the girls knew and used to peek through the door to the pool that was in the main corridor.

I can see that eliminating the need for swim suits meant everyone would go swimming, and the absence of a bathing suit wouldn't save you. However, the girls were swimming in the pool, with bathing suits.

The rock group Lynyrd Skynyrd actually named themselves after a sadistic gym teacher named Leonard Skinner, who died a few years ago.

But the gym teachers I worked with at Woodside were great. John Taylor, an African-American who taught a course for physical educators at Stanford that I really enjoyed, went on to head the teacher training program at Stanford, and, ultimately, became Dean of the School of Education at Arizona State. John was someone who I looked to as a model for what I wanted to be as a teacher.

But Masconomet returned me to Woody Allen's prophecy.

There was the gym teacher and wrestling coach who some of my honors students labeled "The Missing Link".

Another gym teacher never showed any inclination to actually exercise herself. That may be because she was so busy smoking. One never approached her without encountering the stench of tobacco.

Then there was the gym teacher who bumped his way into the English department, when he was laid off as a gym teacher. He found the experience so stressful that he started calling in sick, and ultimately used his sick days rather than continue teaching English. He got a medical excuse to keep him out, which really pissed Dr. Brown off.

That idea stayed with me. I guess not all of the Masco gym teachers were dumb.

Not all meetings are soul-numbing, and faculty meetings could sometimes be interesting. But it didn't help that they would come at the end of the day. Usually, they would be in the library, where the late day sun streaming produced a soporific effect on participants.

As did the sonorous tones of most principals. Worse, they would sometimes want to demonstrate that they had been to a conference, or actually done some professional reading. This would be readily evident once they used a "magic word". These were buzzwords that were intended to show that they were very familiar with the cutting edge of educational innovation. To fully display their magic, these words would need to be repeated numerous times in the course of a single meeting. It became tradition to start counting number of usages in a meeting once any word was used more than once. There may have been some wagering involved.

For one principal, as a former typing teacher, he tended to obsess over the magic word "technology." I remember sitting next to a young teacher who had just been told that he was being laid off. He commented on how unfortunate that staff would have to be reduced.

But he brightened considerably when he described how the new copy machines we would be getting would be a huge step forward for the school.

This was little consolation to the competent math teacher next to me.

Tony was a brilliant, intense English teacher. He also was more interesting than most of my colleagues. He would be the first male teacher at Masco to get an ear pierced, although he never drew any attention to it. He particularly avoided drawing attention to his interest in the paranormal. He shared with me, however, that he used to do hypnosis for MUFON, to gather information from people who might have been abducted by aliens.

I was grateful that Tony was on the faculty, because he was very demanding of his students, which kept me from being a singular lightning rod.

Tony would get to school before most of our colleagues, and buckle down to work at his desk. He was demanding of himself, as well as his students.

Ironically, although Tony was willing to put in extra hours in the morning, the contractual end of the school day was sacred to him. Faculty meetings could drone on far past the contractually allowed time, but Tony would get up at the precise second and walk out.

All of his colleagues were grateful for this, since it did serve as a signal to the principal that a torture session was over. This meant we could escape the long-winded laments of Alvin, the Social Studies teacher for whom whining was as autonomic as breathing. Alvin would stand up in the meetings and begin his recitation of a perceived injustice with a lengthy "Steeeeeeeeeeeeve………………"

We always hoped he would keel over from a lack of oxygen at that point, but he seemed to have some sort of rebreathing technique to sustain him.

But I digress.

So, one day, we arrived before the meeting to see a workman leaving after having installed a new system intended to detect the theft of books, or magazines, or, once a year, the swimsuit issue of Sports Illustrated[116].

The head librarian at the time was young, and pretty hip[117]. She proudly showed us how the bar inserted into a book could be demagnetized at checkout, and students would exit through a metal detector without setting off a shrieking alarm.

---

[116] When they ran their first ever topless model, it was out the door in a heartbeat.

[117] This was not a high bar to get over at Masconomet.

Andy was probably the person who first saw the potential this represented. We hatched a plan, and the librarian gleefully agreed to participate.

When Tony came in, the librarian indicated that she had some new books to show him. While she took him off into the stacks, Andy grabbed Tony's briefcase and hid one of the new security rods within it.

Then we sat back and waited.

Word spread through the faculty as the meeting proceeded. One could tell someone had just received the word when an individual rose up out of their normal slouch, looked over at Tony and grinned broadly.

Perhaps Alvin was not there, but as the contractual witching hour approached, the unexpected happened.

It appeared that Steve was going to wind things up early, and let us leave well before the time when Tony would make his very public stage exit.

Just as Steve was about to dismiss us, I leapt to my feet and asked, "Steve, how can we interface the new technology with our curriculum?"

As Steve began to launch into a stem-winding answer, sighs of relief were audible. Some may actually have been gasps at my having executed an elusive triple magic word score.

Eyes shifted from the clock, to Tony, and back again as the magic moment approached.

On the second, Tony stood up. People moved to the edge of their seats as he approached the metal detector.

Then he passed through it.

And nothing happened.

Steve looked puzzled as groans arose from all parts of the room.

Tony looked back over his shoulder, equally puzzled, but never broke stride as he raced out the door.

I turned to the head librarian, threw up my hands and exclaimed, "Suppose he'd been a terrorist!"

This time, colleagues followed Tony's lead and got up and headed out the door, looking greatly disappointed.

Faced with the exodus, Steve quickly wrapped things up and dismissed the meeting.

Attendance was up at the next faculty meeting.

————————————————————

Nick was a big, strong guy, having played football at Dartmouth. He started at Masco teaching Social Studies to the lowest level kids, and would end up moving into Special Education, where he would again be encountering much of the same population. He was often pretty low affect, and rarely seemed to get very agitated.

One day, in my last years at Masco, I heard Nick in the computer room next to my chemistry class. Perhaps the doors were open, because I could hear Nick very clearly.

And based on his rising volume, he was really angry.

When I heard him say to a student that he was really being "an asshole", I headed to the doorway of the computer room. Nick stood close to the students he was berating, towering over him threateningly. I got Nick's attention and motioned to him to join me in the hallway.

Once we were out of the earshot of kids, I said "I thought you might want to calm down."

The color passed from his face, and he actually blanched as he realized what had happened. He said, "Thanks," and returned to the computer room.

The next morning, he came to me and said, "I wanted to thank you. You probably saved my job yesterday."

I said, "No big deal. I'm sure you would do the same for me."

Not all of the students who took my chemistry class were adolescents.

Sue had taken it after I'd had her sister Ellen in my first year of teaching and Ellen had done well. As I remember it, Sue had left high school without following the path directly to college. She loved horses, and had worked with them after high school. In her early twenties, she decided to go on to college, maybe with an eye to being a veterinarian, and as a result, she wanted to brush up on her chemistry. Like her sister Ellen, Sue could get frustrated and burst into tears over the material, but she was bright and ultimately succeeded in the class.

Terry was in her late thirties when she decided to go to nursing school. She had been a hall monitor at Masco, and knew me as a colleague and knew my reputation as a teacher from talking with the kids. I really admired her determination in coming to my class at her age, and surrounded by kids she had been asking for hall passes for the past few years. Terry found the class hard, and could break into tears herself, but was reasonably successful with the material.

Katie never burst into tears, but she just seemed kinda tough. She was in her mid-twenties when the assistant principal brought her to meet me. He had told me beforehand that she'd had a difficult past, and I didn't inquire about why she was taking my class at that point in her life. She was attractive, so I guessed maybe she had gotten pregnant in high school and dropped out. Given my success with the two adults earlier in my career, it made sense for her to be in my class.

The kids in the class did kinda look at her funny, but she looked distinctly older than they did, which Sue hadn't, and she was not familiar to them, as Terry had been.

Each of the three women had really revved up my idealism. The discussion about women in science had been going on for years, and I naturally favored them as disadvantaged in science by cultural bias. Furthermore, I so admired each of them for having the courage to return to a class surrounded by high school students.

So, while I like to think I gave every students my best, I worked particularly hard for each of them.

I remember that I always put an encouraging comment on Katie's homework, and really focused on her in class to see if she was getting things. I saw her after school at least a couple of times, and gave her pep talks each time.

So I was crestfallen when she came to me in late October and said she wouldn't be coming to class anymore. She had been doing fine, so I gave her another pep talk, on not giving up, etc. The look on her face didn't make sense to me as I tried to rally her.

Katie said that she wasn't giving up, and that I eventually would understand.

I was disappointed in my failure to keep Katie in my class, and said so to the assistant principal the next day.

That was when I learned that Katie wasn't a woman in science.

She was a woman in law enforcement.

Katie had been working undercover in my class. Unbeknownst to me, one of the other students was a major drug dealer. He had an apartment of his own, a car, and quite a clientele, apparently. Katie hadn't succeeded in taking him down, but he disappeared from the school some months later. She had busted at least one other small dealer. After she left, my kids were amused that I hadn't seen the transparency of her cover. Perhaps my idealism blinded me to reality.

Katie called me some months after she left. She apologized for misleading me, and said she had appreciated how hard I had worked for the fictitious character she presented. She said she had never worked so hard in school before that, and that she often had her mother trying to help her on her homework.

She said something I still cherish: "I see what you are trying to do with these kids." Katie told me that she actually worked in the new state prison that had just been built in Middleton, and that she would really like to give me a tour, to thank me for my efforts.

So, at the end of that school year, a tough one in the middle of The Great War, I went to prison. I was accompanied by a supporter in my struggles against Dr. Brown, a parent, friend and prominent community member named Bob Forney. Ironically, Bob had worked undercover for me, gathering information at the school committee about what Dr. Brown was doing.

The prison was really impressive. Sparkling in its' newness, with great exercise facilities for the inmates and food service so good that we had lunch, it was cutting edge in penal institutions.

It also was so clear to me how impossible it would be, if you were trying to escape.

At that point of the year, I was exhausted, trying to survive Masconomet.

Escaping it would have to wait a while longer.

The ABC program at Masco started the same year I began teaching there. I was drawn to the program, and the kids, immediately. The kids lived in a house the program had purchased in Topsfield, and went to the homes of host families in the community a couple of weekends a month.

The ABC students were a social experiment. A Better Chance was a national program, born out of the liberalism of the Sixties and Seventies. It took students who applied from inner city schools to suburban schools, to provide better education and safer environments.

Well-intended though it was, it was triage. The environments and schools left behind required more commitment than the nation could muster to save them, but a fortunate few would get an opportunity to succeed.

I played basketball at Phillips Exeter with a kid named Eddie Perry. A black kid from New York, Eddie still brought the street with him to his game at Phillips Exeter. Eddie was different from other minority kids at Exeter in that he was clearly clinging to some of the culture of his home.

Before he would have gone off to Stanford, Eddie was killed in New York City when he and his brother apparently tried to rob someone who turned out to be a plainclothes cop. There was considerable furor over the killing, not because the shooting of an unarmed black man was unusual, but because Eddie seemed like he had made it out. Michael Jackson designed the video for his song "Bad" around the Eddie Perry story- a kid caught between two worlds[118].

When Jackie Robinson entered the major leagues, he had to endure racist taunts and degradation. He is looked back upon as a hero and a pioneer for what he endured.

He was 28 years old.

But the ABC program was bringing in kids. In the first month of the program, several boys were dismissed and sent home. A local girl, who it was said had claimed she would end the ABC program, had sex with the boys at a dance. She first told a school monitor about it, and the incident was effectively hushed up.

---

[118] As soon as I heard of Eddie's death, I remembered his street posturing at the Academy. I'd thought that, within the culture of the Academy, he seemed like kind of a jerk, but that wasn't reason enough for his life to be extinguished.

At least one other ABC student would be dismissed over the next decade, again for having sex. His judgment was perhaps worse. He convinced a not terribly bright girl to give him oral sex, in a darkened corner at the end of a corridor in the school. It wasn't completely darkened, as there was a window to the outside, through which the boys' cross country team observed the dalliance as they ran by.

I repeat, these were just kids. To expect an adolescent boy to pass up sex, because of the long term goal of education, was ridiculous. But that's what they were being told to do.

I immediately gravitated to the ABC kids. At Phillips Exeter summer session, I had hung with the first black kids I'd gone to school with. At UNH, I went to the parties the black kids held on the dorm floor where many of them lived. In an act of solidarity that did not go unnoticed by my chemistry professor, I remained seated with them during the national anthem before a basketball game.

So having the ABC program made Masco a much more appealing place for me.

I went over to the ABC house often. I would play basketball in the driveway with the kids, or just hang out with them. I remember sitting in dorm rooms at the ABC house, listening to Richard Pryor records I'd brought. While Pryor didn't speak to my personal experience, he did speak to the life the kids were leaving behind to be there[119].

Judy and I would have the ABC kids up to the house in Exeter. Sometimes it would be for a party, to which I'd invite other of my students. For several years, we had the ABC kids up to stay overnight.

To the ABC kids, the big, old wooden house was a foreign experience. Virtually all of them would ask if it was haunted. Although there was enough space for everyone to have a room of their own, they virtually always refused to sleep without company. If one got up in the middle of the night to go to the bathroom, he'd wake his roommate for company on the harrowing trip to the facilities.

After the first year we had them up, the students who were returning would lead the newest students on tours of the house. They, of course, emphasized the haunted nature of the house for maximum effect.

The kids would stay up late, talking, and, occasionally, prowling around the house. One night, I got a great idea, and went to the unfinished room on the third floor. There I grabbed a dress form that my wife and mother used to tailor dresses on.

When the next group of ABC kids approached the room, I opened the door and threw the dress form out.

---

[119] And, he was hysterical. Listening to material considered so vulgar at the time with students was probably a bad idea. If so, it certainly was but one of many bad ideas I would have.

Milton, a big, burly kid who starred on the basketball team, fell to the floor, as the other kids ran. Milton clutched at his sides and wailed, "Oh, God, Oh, God, Oh, God!"

I, of course, was convulsed by this. It seemed less humorous later, when Milton told me that his first impulse had been to throw himself out the third story window, to save himself from the ghost.

In future years, the dress form stayed put.

The turnover among the couples who acted as ABC house parents was pretty high. Judy and I actually talked about doing that job once, when there was a vacancy. I have no doubt that we were fortunate not to have done that. Masco had more than enough stress as it was, and our young marriage might not have survived. Since that marriage would prove crucial to my own Masconomet survival, I'm grateful not to have become the house parents.

I did fund-raisers for ABC with the kids at Masco, and sat on the ABC Board. One year, I went with one of our Spanish teachers, to New York and New Jersey, to interview potential candidates for the program. The prep school assessment tests, SSAT, tended to give us candidates with scores in the bottom ten percentile, so they weren't useful at evaluating candidates. The essays from applicants, interviews and recommendations weren't much more help.

So I waded into the inner city, to meet the kids on their home grounds. There were kids who had looked acceptable in the application process who, upon meeting them, clearly could not have fit in at Masco.

I don't remember if that class of ABC students was any stronger than any other.

I do remember how different the world of the candidates felt, when I was actually there.

Two worlds.

Both Teds would commit suicide, but I only had an inkling about one of them, and the other blindsided me.

One Ted had grown up in the shadow of his older brother. The older brother was senior class president, a good student, and got along well with the adults at Masco. Ted probably heard about that every step of the way through the school system.

So he worked to carve out his own identity, different than his brother. He never made much of an effort in school, although his quick wit was sign that he was intelligent. He achieved his greatest notoriety for his Mick Jagger imitation at Senior Frolics, crotch-grabbing included.

I had encountered him in study halls and hallways through his time in high school. His reputation for difficult behavior preceded him, and I am sure we clashed when I had the prison guard duty that monitoring study halls represented.

He was a senior when I finally had Ted in class. He needed an English course for graduation, and Words on Parade fit the bill. While he was with other potential troublemakers in that class, neither he nor any of the others were a great problem.

He did seem like a pretty unhappy kid. He could be sullen, however, and looked angry at the world at other times.

Maybe it was a cry for attention, or help, as he graffitied "Tedman" all over the school, with the Batman insignia surrounding it. Since everyone knew who was doing it, the fact that he kept it up probably should have been a clue.

He also tagged "Tedman loves Lisa" everywhere. They were together during junior and senior year, and then, midway through senior year, they broke up.

As graduation approached, word spread that Ted might not be graduating. It wasn't clear what he would do after high school, since he didn't seem inclined to go to college- as his brother had done.

He had grown much quieter after he broke up with Lisa. High school provided a structure, and a context, even if it was just one to rebel against.

The call came to the assistant principal in May. The father, who had undoubtedly spent plenty of time working with the assistant principal dealing with his son, said Ted had been taken to the hospital, and he didn't think he'd be coming home. Ted had gone into the garage, attached a hose to the exhaust pipe, and crawled into a sleeping bag, awaiting the end.

In dying, he became, however briefly, something of an icon in the school. He probably would have cherished that.

Fortunately, no copycats followed him.

The other Ted was a very different person. He had been a top student in my journalism class, a positive and upbeat kid to be around. He was always polite, and kind to others.

It had been his idea to invite his father to class when we were going to interview the editor of the Christian Science Monitor. Ted's family was Christian Scientist. Perhaps the religion's views about traditional medicine prevented him from seeking help with a struggle that was never evident to me.

But, one day a year or two after he had graduated, one of my trusted secretaries in the office called. She knew I really liked him, and would want to know.

Ted had killed himself.

I was staggered. I talked with each of my classes that day, to reiterate what I hoped they already knew. They were not alone, they could always call me, reach out in despair, rather than capitulating.

One of my kids said she had seen Ted the day before he died. He was walking down the street, smiling, as he always was. No one saw this one coming.

Two Teds, both dead by their own hand.

I can understand suicide. In despair, illness, loneliness, death could look very inviting.

And suicide can be a final act of lashing out. Gloria Vanderbilt's son, Anderson Cooper's brother, called his mother out to the balcony to witness as he stepped off the edge of their high-rise. Larry Bird's tortured father called his wife on the phone so she would hear as the gun went off.

I have a guess about what was in the heart of the first Ted when he killed himself.

I don't have a guess about the second one.

Only they could know.

And they were both gone.

————————————————————

Mickey was gay. He never came right out and said it to me, but he made it obvious. He had come to Masco in his junior year, and the reason he showed up then wasn't absolutely clear, but he was clearly coming from a difficult situation.

I always reached out to new kids. Having moved three times while I was in school, I knew what it felt like to be the new kid, to have to start fresh in making a whole new set of friends. I'd try to get other kids to reach out to new kids, and I always let them know they could come to me if they were having trouble adjusting.

Mickey confided in me that he had gay friends, and that he had done a lot of clubbing in the city. He may have heard that I was gay, which was a rumor that had been circulated periodically by kids who wanted to get back at me for one thing or another[120].

I didn't ask Mickey if he was trying to tell me if he was gay. I just worked at making him feel accepted, and that I liked him for the nice, gentle kid he was.

Within months, Mickey had moved on again, for reasons unknown to me.

Mickey was one of the reasons I went to the first organizational meeting for the Gay Straight Alliance[121]. I also had been hearing for some time that gay youth were much more likely to commit suicide.

---

[120] To the best of my knowledge, I'm not gay. Not that there's anything wrong with that. And, of course, at least one of my best friends is gay.

[121] Another was the heightened awareness of gay issues that came from a friend who was lesbian. I really worked hard to understand her world. She once said I could be an "honorary lesbian". That meant a lot to me. John Taylor had once said to me that I "should have been a brother." I guess that gave me two merit badges, neither of which are likely to be issued by the Boy Scouts anytime soon.

I was the only teacher at the meeting, although the superintendent, Dr. Cavanaugh, was there also. When a reporter asked why I was there, I said the reason was that I wanted to support kids at risk.

I didn't want to lose any more of my students to suicide.

Suzy wanted to have sex with her boyfriend, and was worried she would get pregnant. This was one of those times when my saying to my classes that they could come to me with anything put me in a position where I didn't have a clue what to say.

I had known Suzy and her boyfriend as a couple for a long time. They were theatre/band kinda kids. Not the kind of kids who I would have thought would be considering sex.

But they were, and Suzy wanted to know if I could help her.

I told her to let me think it over, and we would talk the next day.

As usual, this meant I would be going home to Judy, and asking her what the hell I should do.

Fortunately, Masco had a really good health teacher at the time. She was in her fifties, but related well to kids, and they trusted her. When I had asked Suzy if she had discussed this issue with her guidance counselor, she had identified him, as a way of indicating how lacking in viability that option was.

So, I went to the health teacher, and asked her if she could provide Suzy with some direction. She told me what options she could present to Suzy, and, when I saw Suzy, I told her she could get what she needed from the health teacher.

For once, it was nice that there was a resource in the school that I could utilize.

Suzy ended up marrying her boyfriend. They went on to be pillars in the community, although Suzy died of cancer recently.

When I read of her unfortunate death, I was proud that, at an important point in her life, I'd been of some help.

Tina wanted to have sex with her boyfriend, but not intercourse. This was somewhat ironic, since the reputation she had from her younger days in high school was of incredible promiscuity.

My opinion of her clearly mattered to her, so maybe the claim that she didn't want to have intercourse was a way of restoring her reputation in my eyes.

Fortunately, I had seen a column in a newspaper addressing adolescents and sex. It was pretty forward thinking for the time, and had discussed alternatives to intercourse, including mutual masturbation.

I was able to point to the column, hanging on a wall above my desk in the prep room.

When I had cut it out, I hadn't envisioned that I would use it, but thought it would be handy if I did need it.

Boy, was I grateful to just be able to hand the column to Tina to read. I know I could not have handled such a topic so gracefully on the spur of the moment.

After that, I wanted to be prepared to give students alternatives.

And, if I could do it with a minimum of talking about it myself, all the better.

Trixie was an ecdysiast.[122]

She was a student in my lowest level chemistry class as a junior. She was an attractive and social young woman who didn't work overly hard in school. I had noticed her at dances as an unusually skilled and enthusiastic dancer.

She provided a preview of her future career during halftime of a football game at Masco. She came out to midfield in a fur, then, to the band's playing "The Stripper", shed clothing down to a bikini.

Richards, who was high school principal at the time, had to be physically restrained by the junior high principal seated next to

---

[122] Using that word, instead of "stripper" or "exotic dancer" is rather pedantic. Research shows 82% of pedants would use "ecdysiast". 91% of pedants use the phrase "research shows" a great deal.

him from running on to the field to stop the shameful display. The band director caught his wrath afterwards, and was not back the next year.

I found out Trixie had given up her amateur status when she picked me up hitchhiking once, after she had been graduated. I was hitching home to Exeter, because my carpool buddies had all chosen to go to the end of the year luncheon. That was a social occasion on which I almost always passed.

Trixie and her friends were in a convertible, with the top (on the car) down, headed for Hampton Beach. She told me that she was dancing at the strip club about 10 minutes down the highway from Masco. I don't remember if she indicated whether she had started there before graduation.

When I began teaching journalism, I was always looking for stories about interesting Masco grads. Trixie certainly fit the bill. Dr. Brown had just begun as superintendent, so he still saw me as an asset. He told me that the school committee had been unhappy with the article on Trixie, but he had defended it.

Everyone should find a profession that works for them.

In the quote that ended the article, Trixie indicated she had done that.

She said, "I just like to dance."

———————————

Alan and Steve were social outliers. They both had rather odd senses of humor, and probably saw me as a fellow traveler. Steve used to work with mentally challenged kids outside of school, perhaps at the State Hospital down the interstate. Steve would mimic one of his clients, saying that the fellow would say "Hi.Hi.Hi.Hi.Hi.Hi.Hi." Steve would say it quickly, with his head tilted to one side, so it did seem amusing. Steve was a bright but odd kid, so his social circle was limited.

Alan was less academically inclined, and turned up in my lower level chemistry class the year after I'd had Steve in College Prep chemistry. Alan was only interested in working on cars, and Masconomet still had an automotive program at that point in the Seventies. Alan's specialty was to say shocking things in moments of silence in class. They weren't obscenities, just words one didn't hear much in common usage. He would break the silence in the classroom by blurting out "Enema!" He derived pleasure if such an utterance would shock a girl in the class. Since he wasn't swearing, or actually harassing anyone, I chose to ignore the outbursts rather than reinforce them by acknowledging them.[123]

Although they were the best friends each one had, they seemed to want to rat one another out in stories they came to tell me. Steve claimed Alan had found some blasting caps at a construction site, and was going to use them for unknown purposes. I got the information from him about where the blasting caps were, and contacted the police.

---

[123] Okay, I thought it was funny, and I hoped it would go away.

I don't know what the consequences were for Alan. But Alan came to me after that, saying that Steve had told him that he was molesting some of the females he was working with at the hospital. He said Steve told him the girls weren't cognizant enough to know what he was doing, so it didn't matter.

I didn't know if Alan was telling the truth, or just making something up because he was angry with Steve. I may never have brought that dilemma home to Judy, because I know I never did anything.

But it stays with me, still.

Patrick was a bully. He had an unusual advantage over Masconomet in that he was a black kid who had grown up in the community. A reputation preceded him, of using allegations of racism when he encountered discipline.

And Patrick did need discipline. When he was still in junior high, I used to see him wandering the halls unfettered. I watched the junior high principal reasoning with Patrick to get him to return to class and saw from the look on Patrick's face that he knew he was gaming the system.

When he was finally in my class, I initially didn't have major problems with him. The racism accusation wasn't going to work with me. I had a long association with the ABC program, and I was friends with the cousin Patrick lived with.

I should have failed Patrick the first time I had him in class. He did virtually no work, but he passed in a final project which, while completely pathetic and late, gave me the justification to give him a D minus. I don't know if that was a good deed[124], but it certainly didn't go unpunished, since I got Patrick back in my class in another year, when he needed to meet a science requirement.

One day, when my back was turned to a difficult class of juniors, I heard something bounce off the blackboard.

I looked on the floor and saw that it was a condom in a wrapper. Kids were snickering, and it wasn't immediately obvious who the culprit was. I told the class that I was going into the room next door, and when I returned, someone had better have picked up the condom, or there would be hell to pay. I went next door, and called the assistant principal to let him know what was going on, and that he would probably be getting a customer soon.

As I stood there, I heard the one senior in the class screaming at someone, "Pick it up!" Shortly afterward, I could hear someone getting up, and the sound of something going into the trashcan.

I returned to class, and, at the end, subtly motioned for the senior to stay. He was a good kid, who was chagrined to be in with some of these clowns. I told him I knew he hadn't done it, and asked him who had.

---

[124] Actually, I do know. It wasn't.

He readily gave up Patrick, and I promised him no one would know that he had been the informant.

Then I spoke to the assistant principal, and told him that I felt what Patrick had done was a form of sexual harassment. If Patrick wasn't removed, I would have to ask the teacher's association to intercede.

Patrick was gone the next day.

But I wasn't through with him. I learned later that Patrick was bullying some of the freshman I taught. They hated it, but were intimidated by a kid who was bigger and older than they were.

So, one day, I was in the weight room with those same freshmen. We were holding what I called the Work Olympics. Since work equals force times distance, we were lifting weights and measuring who could do the most work.

Most of my kids had recorded their efforts, when Patrick sauntered into the room. He wasn't with a class, but just wandering, as was his wont to do.

I told the kids it was my turn, to see if I could outwork them. I bench-pressed all the weight on the machine. Then I said, "Hey Patrick, let's see what you can do."

He declined.

I asked him again, saying that certainly he had to be stronger than me.

He declined again, as the kids whom he had been tormenting started to look at one another and grin.

When I asked him one more time, this time clearly taunting him, he left the weight room.

The next day, the assistant principal told me Patrick had been to see him. Patrick had said he didn't want me to talk to him anymore. The assistant principal, clearly relishing the irony, suggested that might be a good idea. I acquiesced, saying it probably wouldn't ever be necessary anyway.

Schools are much better now about preparing faculty in how to deal with bullying.

I didn't have any of that preparation. I probably should have been more sensitive to the factors that led Patrick to be a bully. I didn't know then how to bring that kind of awareness into play. However, I do know that Patrick's ability to act as a bully to my kids stopped that day in the weight room.

Barry was an extortionist. The custodian for my room came to me, and told me that there was a big football player who was asking junior high kids for money during their lunch. The cafeteria workers had let him know, and he thought I was most likely to put a stop to it.

The school year was barely underway. However, I knew Barry because he was in my chemistry class. So I asked him that day to stay after class, and asked him if he had been taking money from junior high kids.

He said he wasn't taking the money; they were giving it to him willingly, when he asked for spare change.

I explained that, because of size and age differential, his requests for spare change were going to be fulfilled, whether the kids really wanted to give him money or not.

I told him to stop, or there would be more trouble for him to follow.

The next day, the custodian came to me during the junior high lunch, and said he was doing it again. I walked across the hall to the cafeteria, and there he was.

I was so pissed I didn't want to deal with it, for fear my emotion would get the better of me.

So I told him to report to the assistant principal's office.

Don, the assistant principal, didn't have a hard-ass reputation- that was why the custodian had come to me.

When I saw Don later in the day, he told me that he, too, had been unable to persuade Barry of the error of his ways. So he told Barry that he was to go home and tell his parents what he had been doing, and discuss it with them.

The next day rolled around, and there was Barry in the cafeteria again.

That evening was Parent's Night, and, to my delight, both of Barry's parents were there.

This time, I asked them to stay after class.

"Are you aware that your son has been taking money from junior high school kids?"

"Yes, we are," responded his dad. "We told him not to do it last night."

"Well, he was doing it again today."

The mother looked chagrined, but the father just shook his head, and even seemed to have the beginnings of a smile.

Now I wasn't holding back.

"You know," I said. "If I had ever done that, and particularly after my parents told me not to, my late father would still be alive today, just so he could be kicking my ass!"

The father blanched, and left saying little.

I figured this would end up a parent complaint that could be used against me, but I didn't care.

The next day, when Barry came to class, he looked somewhat chagrined, and somewhat annoyed with me.

I never heard anything about a complaint, and Barry wasn't seen in the junior high lunch again.

———————————————————

Kerry was "a competitive hip-hop dancer." It was an unusual self-description at the start of the year, not just for a freshman girl, but within the rather Caucasian culture of Masconomet. However, I knew I was still Motown, and rap had long ago passed me by. Maybe the community was changing, and I wasn't.

Kerry wasn't a great student. When I began my system of allowing students who had received A's on the last test to come to class late and sit wherever they wished, she was resentful. On the next test, she received a C. That really annoyed her, because she had studied for it with her closest friend in the class.

That closest friend was probably not the best study partner. She was not a particularly good student herself. But the two girls were friends, and somewhat removed from the rest of the class.

There was one kid in the class who was kind of an outsider. He wasn't really sharp himself, just a nice kid who was probably a little less mature than his classmates. In class one day, the hip hop dancer mocked him in front of the whole class.

Outraged by the bullying, I called her outside the class. After I closed the door, I read her the riot act. She passed off her actions as inconsequential, claiming she was actually friends with her target, and that he wouldn't mind.

Within a few days, I saw her in the hallway, accompanied by a group of her friends.

She said to me "I'm going to get you. I'm going to be a lawyer, and I'll get you."

I was puzzled, but didn't think much more at the time. I'd been threatened before, particularly by Jenny, who mentioned guns twice.

So Kerry's comment didn't really register with me. This seemed more like a joke than a threat.

Chapter 17

Step Away from the Chalkboard

Once Dr. Brown "retired" from the superintendency, the waters smoothed significantly for me. I knew there were whispering campaigns about me- I'd heard all sorts of stuff almost as long as I'd been there. I knew that the creepiest of kids I'd dealt with were capable of anything, and just brushed it off as the price of doing things in the ways I believed were right.

Richards's lame duck two years didn't produce any more strife.

But, after Dr. Cavanaugh came as superintendent, and I started to inquire about another sabbatical, things began to get weird.

She had initially been very encouraging about the sabbatical. But she seemed cool to the idea as the application moved forward.

This was about the same time that my basketball buddy Dave and I went to her office because she had told him there had been a harassment complaint. Dave had asked me if someone about whom a complaint had been filed should be asked if they wanted to hear about it, even if the complaint wasn't going to move forward. I had said yes, then was dumbfounded when he said the complaint had been about me.

So we went to Dr. Cavanaugh's office, and got nothing. She never identified the nature of the complaint, or the complainant, and said the complainant had not proceeded with it, because she liked me. We walked out wondering what was going on.

That same school year, a young math teacher whose name I didn't know[125] showed me an email note to her that purported to be from me. It was what used to be called a "mash note", using florid language that would have embarrassed me if I had written it[126]. At that point, I didn't even use email, except when Judy was there to help me.

The math teacher and I went over our class rosters, and found one computer-savvy student who seemed like a possible culprit. He denied up and down that it was him. And, some weeks later, he came to me to ask if I had any computer files at Masco under my name. At that point, Judy hadn't shown me yet how to create a file, and I was only using Masco computers to input grades and create tests. The student told me that the files under my name were graphic, with headings like "Lubricants".

I figured it was just another student trying to hurt me. Still, I really wanted to get away from the moral cesspool that Masco felt like.

But, at the school committee, the support that had seemed solid for my sabbatical seemed to have evaporated.

---

[125] And still don't remember.
[126] It started off "My little Southern belle………………………." I wouldn't have written that to a female when I was in junior high school.

Dr. Cavanaugh, who had also been very encouraging earlier in the year when I told her I wanted to speak at graduation, now seemed unsupportive of that idea, too.

So, when the sabbatical was rejected, I put in for the two year change of career leave that was in the contract, and looked forward to leaving Masco, hopefully for good. For the rest of the year, being at Masco made me physically uncomfortable.

I spent the next two years at MIT. Being at a world class institution, where I was treated as a valued resource, served to highlight the absurdity of what I had endured at Masco.

Sometime during those two years I stopped at Masco for something or other. I learned that math teacher Alan Hand had left, under somewhat mysterious circumstances.

While I was there, the assistant principal came up to me and asked if I knew why Hand had left.

Now why would I, of all people, know the answer to that? This was the only time in two years I'd stopped in. I'd even stopped participating in morning basketball, although it continued without me. So why was he asking me?

I started doing research on Alan, and found he had been charged with possessing child pornography and contacting a minor for sex through the Internet. Unfortunately, or fortunately, it was a sting operation and Alan was indicted.

That night, I sat up bolt upright in the middle of the night.

Alan Hand had been using my name!

That explained the mash note, the file, and probably whatever withdrawn complaint Dave and I had been to Dr. Cavanaugh's office to learn nothing about. If Dr. Cavanaugh had revealed anything at that time, much of what Hand had apparently done afterward might have been prevented[127].

Now I wanted to verify that he had used my name.

So I went to the FBI and put in a request to see the case file, explaining that I wanted to see if Hand had used my name.

The request was denied. They cited "privacy issues".

So whose privacy were they protecting?

Certainly not mine.

So, when I returned to Masco, that unknown remained.

I was given an awful room, one basically not equipped for the science classes I had been assigned. And the class assignments

---

[127] There are laws protecting accusers in harassment cases, but the accused lacks protection against false claims. A few years before, I'd overheard one of my most difficult students talking to a friend who was really angry with her parents. She had recommended that her friend file an abuse claim with the state as a reprisal, even though there was no validity to the claim.

were no bargain, either. Ironically, Lee gave me one of the few computers assigned to an individual teacher, which I figured was because I used the computer to create tests.

I learned that colleagues at Masco were really unnerved by what happened to Alan Hand, just as they had been when Dr. Brown had fired Jay.

But this went even further. Dr. Cavanaugh was credited with going so far as to see that Hand was stripped of his pensions- both school and National Guard. In casual conversation, Alan had identified his retirement date to me before I left for the two years.

Now he was on probation, an identified sex offender, and all of that retirement money he had contributed to and worked for was gone. He worked as a groundskeeper at a golf course.

We were told on the first day of the year about an ongoing investigation into child abuse in the community, and to make sure that no references to it occurred in our classes- not by us or students. Another veil of silence.

The culture of the faculty was very different upon my return. People who had fought Dr. Brown, and Dr. Cavanaugh, and had fought union battles, like Dave, and four of the reactionary math department, were gone. Of people who historically would stand up and speak up, whether out of principle or just oppositional nature, there was only one left- me. The union was headed by a milquetoast Spanish teacher, and the head of the PIC, through which any grievances ran, was Nick.

I sent a memo to Dr. Cavanaugh as soon as school started, expressing my concerns that Hand had used my name. The only response I got from her was when she sidled up to me before a faculty meeting and told me I didn't have anything to worry about. I didn't understand initially what she was referencing, but she gave enough clarification that I eventually figured she was referring to the Hand case. That would be the only time she ever responded to my inquiry, and she made sure she did it when no one else was around, and not in writing.

Maybe Paxil just makes the world rosy, but I was enjoying myself, despite being put in lousy teaching conditions. By the end of October, the only disciplinary action I'd taken was chewing out the "competitive hip-hop dancer" for verbally bullying her classmate.

A few days later, I was teaching about perspective and parallax in front of class. As a metaphor, I suggested how a student and I might look at the hip-hop girl's hair and describe it as being two different colors.

A boy in class said "How would you know what color her hair really is?"

I looked down at the table in front of me, buying time. Was he making a vulgar joke? These were just freshman. I was concerned that I had drawn unneeded attention to the girl's hair, and that alone might embarrass her, not to mention if she saw crude intent in his comment.

Flustered, I said, "Let's not go there," and changed the subject.

I didn't think any more about it.

A few days later, I noticed that the hip hop girl and her one friend in the class were absent. Students in class pointed out their absence, as if they knew something was going on. I saw the two students through the window as they went by outside the class with a female gym teacher. I figured they were working with her on a project, and the teacher would let me know why she had kept them out of class.

It may have been later the same day that the superintendent's secretary called and told me I was to report to the superintendent's office after school. It was a Friday, and I was going down to the Cape for a conference with a friend who had just addressed my freshman on the topic of women in science.

I told the secretary that I wouldn't be coming over, since I had to leave for the Cape. She called back and was insistent that I had to come to Dr. Cavanaugh's office.

I knew that was outside of contractual hours and I could refuse, but my friend Lynda, who had been in charge of legal affairs at Exeter, said we should go and find out what was going on.

When we got to Dr. Cavanaugh's office, Dr. Post, my department head, was there. Dr. Cavanaugh handed me a letter saying that I was suspended, pending an investigation of allegations. Having faith in Lynda's legal expertise, I let her do the talking. She pushed Dr. Cavanaugh hard to find out the allegations, but got nothing. Dr. Cavanaugh maintained that informing me of the allegations would compromise the investigation.

We left the office. I wasn't worried, since I knew I had done nothing[128]. Lynda was worried, however. For all I knew, she was speaking from experience when she said "They must think you raped someone."

Then I was worried, but it still seemed absurd.

Lynda and I cancelled the trip to the Cape. I tried to contact the union president and the grievance chair in the school building, but they had left.

We went home and told Judy. She was deeply concerned. Judy had known Dr. Cavanaugh when they worked in the same district in New Hampshire. When I was investigating her as a candidate for the Masco superintendency, Judy had the only words of concern anyone expressed. She had said at the time "Don't trust her."

Judy's worries now really concerned me. Facing the unknown, it was easy to imagine the worst.

We contacted a lawyer. When I had first gone to the school committee in the grievance process with Dr. Brown, we had

---

[128] Again, maybe that was the Paxil. The brand name comes from the Latin "Pax", for peace. My guard wasn't just down; I'm not sure I had one at that point.

brought an expensive lawyer. The union had also sent a legal advisor at that time, who had roared at Dr. Brown and the school committee, rendering the expensive lawyer unnecessary from that point on. But this seemed potentially even more serious, so we hired a lawyer Lynda recommended before we were even able to get hold of the union representatives.

The weekend was horrible. Saturday morning, I found out that Judy had not slept. Having seen Masconomet in action, she conjured up the worst scenarios possible. That, in turn, made me enormously anxious and upset.

We talked with the union president over the weekend. Judy was talking with him on the phone when he said to her "Dr. Cavanaugh feels she can do whatever she wants."

Judy's response was "That's because you let her!"

On Monday morning, our lawyer called to say he had spoken with Masco's lawyer. He learned that the basis for the information seemed to be a student complaining that my comment in the hair color discussion was sexual harassment. The lawyer for the district was even conveying that it didn't seem to be that big an issue.

When our lawyer told me over the phone what the basis for the suspension was, I felt as if my head would explode. I told the lawyer to hang on for a second, covered the phone and swore at the top of my lungs[129]. Then I uncovered the phone to continue talking with the lawyer.

Although the district lawyer had indicated that it was not such a huge issue, the investigation would continue, and I was to report to the superintendent's office on Thursday. Dr. Brown had had his fishing expedition, now it was Dr. Cavanaugh's turn.

When the meeting came on Thursday, the union president and Nick came, but with no legal support. The union rules stated that if a union member chose to hire an attorney, the union was not obligated to provide any legal support. Years earlier, against Dr. Brown, the union had opted to provide support, perhaps because of their animus against Dr. Brown. This time, I was on my own.

There wasn't much expansion of the allegations. The "hip hop dancer" had been joined by her one friend in the class. They were two of the only three students who weren't performing at the A or B level in classroom testing; the other was the very kid the dancer had verbally bullied.

The second student's complaint was that once, when she had been staring absently out the window during class, I had stopped talking to the class until they were all looking at her, and then closed the blinds in front of her.

The description of my comment had been enhanced now to have me saying "let's not go <u>down</u> there", which I supposedly

---

[129] At that point, the Paxil was as overwhelmed pharmaceutically as I was emotionally.

followed with a look down to my "pubic region"[130]. The gym teacher who had brought them to Dr. Cavanaugh complained that I had made an offensive joke in a conversation with her and the girls' varsity basketball coach. All of the students in the class had been interviewed, and perhaps others, although that was not clear.

And that's all they had.

A perfectly good fishing expedition, wasted.

Through all of this, the two union members had sat silent, in fact, close to inanimate. If my rights were going to be trampled, they either could or would not see it.

Dr. Cavanaugh said I could return to the classroom, and that she cleared me of harassment, although she said my students felt that my comment was sexual harassment. Since she had interviewed every student in that class, she gave the impression that this was the wide consensus.

She did say that, to protect the privacy of the complainants, I was not to discuss this with anyone in school. Oh, and that I should "be careful."

So I returned to school with a cloud of mystery and suspicion over me. That was verified within a day, when I saw a memo to all the members of the science department from Dr. Post,

------

[130] Their words, not mine.

telling them that, while he couldn't share the details, the allegations against me hadn't been anywhere as bad as the worst rumors circulating.

One of the secretaries in the office told me that a student in one of my classes had shared with her the worst rumors, and she had told him they were untrue, and to stop saying that.

Under such circumstances, I found being back in school was enormously stressful. I started having the nurse check my blood pressure during the day. Having always been 120/80, it was now dangerously high each day.

After a few days, I realized one morning on my ride in that I couldn't do this anymore. I pulled over on the side of the interstate and sat leaning on the steering wheel, sobbing.

I knew I was done, unless things changed dramatically.

First, I couldn't have my health jeopardized. My first responsibility was to Judy, and staying healthy was key to fulfilling that in the decades we had ahead of us.

Second, a key to effective classroom leadership and discipline is moral stature. Over the years, I had become, relative to a declining school culture, more and more of an old guard disciplinarian. It seemed impossible to do that if students were eying me as some kind of pervert in their midst.

So I told my students in each class that day that I found that being there was jeopardizing my health, and I wasn't coming back as long as that was the case.

I had the longest talk with the freshman class where the complaint had arisen. The two girls were no longer there, having been moved to another class, which was probably one of their objectives. The kids remaining in the class said the two girls had called them soliciting support in the complaint, but they hadn't gone along with it.

The kids described how they had each been called over to Dr. Cavanaugh's office and interviewed. (This was done without notifying parents, as was required in such investigations.) They thought they, themselves, were in trouble when they got to the superintendent's office, which was a totally unfamiliar place to them.

I told them that I was sorry they had seen my comment as harassment, since I had always emphasized to them the importance of being respectful of others.

They erupted in protest, saying they had never said they thought I had been harassing anyone. One of them even said that the superintendent had lied if she told me that.

I wished them the best, and told them they weren't likely to see me again, given the untenable circumstances I had been placed in.

My last view of Masco on that day was the way the school looked best- in my rear view mirror.

I saw my physician, who was supportive, and I began calling in sick.

While I was out, I got a threatening email from the address dunnandead01@yahoo.com. It said I should not return to Masco, or else.

I contacted the school and asked that they investigate. The response I got was that Lee had checked the computer in my room, and it hadn't come from there. Apparently, they were verifying that I hadn't sent it to my home email from school.

I later learned there was a clue in the email that pointed to the sender. In the text, as a stand-alone sentence, was a single word: "Recognize." Listening to a record by Prince much later, I would learn that this term was used in hip-hop culture, although I don't know its' exact implication.

While I was out, Judy and I sent a letter to the principal, figuring perhaps she was in a position to defuse the situation and make my return possible. We said all she had to do was put out a letter to the school saying that I had been accused and found not guilty.

They were never willing to do that.

And so the door to the teaching profession closed to me forever.

When I started writing this chapter, I thought it might be cathartic. However, having done it, I find I haven't undergone any catharsis.

That may be because I don't find myself angry at anyone. While there are people I've spoken of in this book for whom I have a healthy dose of contempt, more than a decade has passed, and I don't think of them, or Masco, very often. And contempt is, unlike anger and hatred, non-corrosive.

The stress and anxiety-filled nightmares that haunted my early years of retirement are now very rare. Ironically, the most common one now has me on the first day of school. I'm about to start teaching the Spanish class I've been assigned. My knowledge of Spanish is limited to Carlos Santana song titles and Taco Bell menu items.

I feel sorry for Alan Hand, whose life was thoroughly ruined, albeit as a result of his own actions. I sent a letter to his home during the first year after I stopped going to Masco. Without anger or rancor, I asked him if he had been using my name.

I never heard back from him.

Since I left Masco, my life has been great. It took some time to shake the anxiety that Masco had imposed upon me. Initially, I went back to MIT and stayed there until I tired of the commute. I wrote a few magazine articles, then two books. I played basketball until I ruptured an Achilles at age 55. For many years, I spent four or five hours a day at the gym, five days a week.

I take care of the house, and I am a good husband.

Judy worked until she retired from New Hampshire, then we moved up to Vermont full-time. She started working part-time in a small K-12 school in a neighboring town, and she continues to love her colleagues and her work.

We both have been blessed by good health, and we say often that we couldn't imagine a life any better.

I continue to take short trips around the country, on the three days when she works. My skiing hasn't improved, but often I'll stop on top of a mountain somewhere, in the middle of a bright sunshine-filled day, and think to myself, "I could be in a classroom at Masco."

And a great day seems even better.

If life was like the movie Groundhog Day-an endless loop of do-overs, then one could make different choices, and new mistakes, each time around.

I'd make the same choices, and the same mistakes, each time, in hopes that my good fortune would continue to return me to the life I have now.

My crusading days are in a distant past.

Made in the USA
Charleston, SC
17 September 2013